The
God
Letters

The God Letters

Edited by
Paul Rifkin

WARNER BOOKS

A Warner Communications Company

In the interest of maintaining the personal flavor of each letter writer, no attempt has been made to correct the grammar, punctuation, or misspellings occuring in the original response letters.

Copyright © 1986 by Paul Rifkin
All rights reserved.
Warner Books, Inc., 666 Fifth Avenue, New York, NY 10103

W A Warner Communications Company

Printed in the United States of America
First Printing: April 1986
10 9 8 7 6 5 4 3 2 1

Book design: H. Roberts

Library of Congress Cataloging-in-Publication Data
Main entry under title:

The God letters.

1. God—Miscellanea. I. Rifkin, Paul.
BT102.G596   1986   211   85-22787
ISBN 0-446-38319-8 (U.S.A.) (pbk.)
     0-446-38320-1 (Canada) (pbk.)

I dedicate this book to my parents,
Sue and Bernie Rifkin,
and to Margie McConnel,
who always emanates the spirit of God.

Contents

AUTHORS   **81**

Introduction

For the first twenty years of my life I was aware mostly of a sense of loneliness, of being alone. All things were distinctly separate, and I was indeed apart from, rather than a part of, all that surrounded me. But then, most miraculously on a holy winter evening in 1965, sparked by the warmth and love of close friends, I became aware of the "energy that connects." An agnostic or atheist until that night, I have never doubted the existence of God since.

This phenomenon included no embodiment. Jesus did not appear...Buddha did not smile...there was neither Moses nor burning bush...Mohammed uttered not a syllable...yet I was infused with a protoplasmic warmth derived from the spirits of all religion. And a new curiosity was born. The excitement I felt gave birth to the project which has eventuated in this book, *The God Letters.*

Yes, I sought to discover how others have come to find and view God. My interest, however, was not academic. In order to cut through any abstraction or self-consciousness, I called on the trickster, the so-called "coyote within." American Indian culture, especially west of the Rocky Mountains (e.g., the Shoshonean and California Indians), bequeathed to modern poetry the heritage of the "Coyote Man"—the trickster hero. This mythic character is a champion of mischief and outrageous acts. His goal, however, is not trickery for its own sake...but for the purpose of teaching...of enlightening. As Gary Snyder points out in *The Old Ways,* the figure of Coyote

Man "in psychological terms, refers to something in ourselves which is creative, unpredictable, contradictory: trickster human nature" (page 75, City Lights Books, 1977). Indeed, the Navajos refer to the coyote as "God's Dog" for its cleverness (e.g., at finding water in the desert).

And so I employed this most overt and active spirit of mischievousness in my soul to evoke heartfelt, unselfconscious replies to the most intimate question I could form: Do you believe in God? And if so, how did God reveal himself? I wrote to prominent people—posing as a fifth-grader doing a school report. And the trick drew forth the moving, unguarded responses which make up this book.

When I wrote again to each respondent revealing my guise and requesting permission to publish, those that said "yea" (often complimenting the "wily" nature of the endeavor) did so from an openness and ability to give of themselves that astonished me. Those that said "nay" (often expressing a loathing and contempt for me and my project) did so with a ferocity that was overwhelming. But as Coyote might say: You play your tricks and take your chances. Strangely, the dichotomy of response actually clarifies the concept of morality...that it most certainly is in the eye of the beholder. As Coyote Man, I am pleased that some found the project delightful, some despicable. And beware, I go now to howl at new moons...to more adventurous trickery...as my God laughs both at me and with me.

The letters in this book are entertaining, inspirational, instructive, humorous, and illuminating. I hope that they will not only reveal views of God and shed light on the character and personality of the respondents, but also that they will help put into focus your own views of God and morality.

Paul Rifkin
May, 1985

DEAR ——— :

I AM making a survey OF FAMOUS people I Respect FOR a 5th Grade class report. My question to you is: DO YOU BELIEVE IN GOD ?? [IF the answer is yes, please describe how God made his presence known to you]. THANK YOU IN Advance FOR YouR answer.

Sincerely,
Paul Rifkin
Grade 5

674 Route 6A
East Sandwich, MA 02537
USA

October 12, 1983

Dear Sir/Madam:

Some time ago I wrote to you and other prominent people around the world inquiring as to your views concerning your belief in God. The questions I posed were: Do you believe in God? And, if so, how did God make himself known to you? My purpose was to gather data on the great variety of ways that people understand and view God. I chose to write in the guise of a fifth-grader in order to obtain sincere, unguarded, "from-the-heart" replies.

The results have been overwhelming. I have a collection of inspiring, educational and often amusing responses. I am planning to publish a book which will compare current significant opinion on this subject with that of earlier centuries. The book will include both the devout and the doubtful:

St. Thomas Aquinas: "Reason in man is rather like God in the world."

Mark Twain: "If there was an all-powerful God, he would have made all good, and no bad."

Herman Melville: "Yea and Nay—Each hath his say: But God He keeps the middle way."

I thank you for your graciousness in responding to my questions. I would like to include your reply along with those of Lee Iacocca, Norman Vincent Peale, Marcel Marceau, Allen Ginsberg and others as representatives of twentieth-century thinking.

Enclosed is a copy of your response. I am requesting your permission to print your reply in my book. Please sign the enclosed grant of permission and return it to me in the self-addressed, stamped envelope. A complimentary copy of the book will be forwarded to you upon publication.

Thank you for your reply.

Sincerely,

Paul Rifkin

PR/gw
Enclosures

The
God
Letters

Entertainers

"And I say to mankind, Be not curious about God.
For I, who am curious about each, am not curious
about God—I hear and behold God in every object,
yet understand God not in the least."

—Walt Whitman
"Leaves of Grass"

October 19, 1980

Dear Paul Rifkin:

Thank you for your letter. Let me try to answer your
question about God.

The miricle is consciousness; the glory is being alive.
The "God" I comprehend is the manifestation of these two.
Regards.

EDWARD ALBEE
Playwright—*Who's Afraid of Virginia Woolf?, A Delicate Balance*

Lion's Gate Films, Inc.

November 9, 1976

Mr. Paul Rifkin
Grade 5
4212 25th St.
San Francisco, CA 94114

Dear Paul:

I do not believe in God because my presence precedes his. Therefore I must assume that he is my creation - and I MUST NOT believe in my own creations or I would be guilty of the authorship of this note.

Sincerely,

Robert Altman

ROBERT ALTMAN
Film director, writer, producer—*M*A*S*H, Nashville, McCabe and Mrs. Miller*

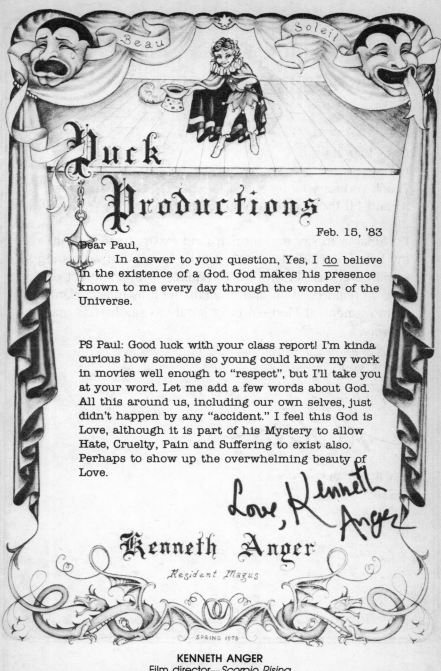

Beau Soleil

Puck Productions

Feb. 15, '83

Dear Paul,

In answer to your question, Yes, I <u>do</u> believe in the existence of a God. God makes his presence known to me every day through the wonder of the Universe.

PS Paul: Good luck with your class report! I'm kinda curious how someone so young could know my work in movies well enough to "respect", but I'll take you at your word. Let me add a few words about God. All this around us, including our own selves, just didn't happen by any "accident." I feel this God is Love, although it is part of his Mystery to allow Hate, Cruelty, Pain and Suffering to exist also. Perhaps to show up the overwhelming beauty of Love.

Love, Kenneth Anger

Kenneth Anger

Resident Magus

SPRING 1975

KENNETH ANGER
Film director—*Scorpio Rising*

edward asner

February 25, 1983

Dear Paul,

Thank you for your letter and for your respect—I appreciate it, and I'll try to answer your question.

I'm unable to say flat out that God exists. I vacillate in my belief, but when I do it's usually because of witnessing some gorgeous act or view of nature, or in some act of God's creatures (man and animal), such as music, dance or movement. If God exists, it is safe to say he has many flowers.

Thank you,

[signature: Ed Asner]

Edward Asner

kk

8-6-83

Mr. Paul Rifkin, Grade 5
East Sandwich, Mass 02537

Dear Paul

Your letter asks two questions. 1. Do I believe in God?
The answer: YES, most definately!   Then:

2. How has He made His presence known to me?

Well, Paul I think all knowledge is obtained by one of four ways:

1. Authority.   This includes the words of those we reasonably can
        believe. It starts with parents and teachers but goes on
        to many eminent and respected persons. It includes books
        of sacred scripture, dictionaries, scientific findings, etc.

2. Rationalism.   This means that the what we allow oursleves to
        believe must be reasonable. In Isaiah 1 : 18 God says, "Let
        us reason together."

3. Intuition.   I cannot explain all the modern theories about how
        some persons seem to have insights to facts that have
        eluded others, nor how so many of the ancient patriarchs
        received great truths by way of dreams and visions. No
        doubt there many areas of the human mind that are still
        a mystery. If or when you have such an experience you
        will know what I am talking about. It will surprise you.

4. Experience, or what science calls: Empiricism.
        We will ultimately, really believe only those things which
        are validated by the facts we encounter in living. As the
        years go on we will treasure the truths which seem to
        have been verified in our lifetime adventure . . . and
        perhaps corroborated by others. But we must not reject
        beautiful teachings simply because they may not seem
        to conform to some of the tragic events we know take
        place. To understand life and to see the hand of God

LEW AYRES
Actor—All Quiet on the Western Front

7

within it takes a great deal of study, thought and patience because, beyond all other problems, you are seeking the most important, and deepest mystery known to mankind. But start with FAITH an DETERMINATION to stick with all the ideals of truth, goodness and beauty. Don't look at only surface evidence but try to comprehend the underlying direction of the universe . . . and mankind . . . not just <u>ourselves</u> or the front pages of the papers.

I have always tried to do that, and believe me Paul, it has paid off. I see many sad things in the world, but I know they are the price of our freedom . . . which MUST BE so that we can grow, mature and become the glory of the universe. Those of us who have a glimpse of the beauty which lies ahead for mankind know that it will be a hard, hard struggle, and many may lose hope along the way. But if we do not become cynical, if we continue to fight for those things which are right and good . . . not just for ourselves or our own little group but for <u>everyone</u> . . . as best as we can know it (and that's never an easy decision) . . . then bit by bit, we will all come closer together, we will solve the stubborn problems which now stand between us. . . . and all mankind will have won the great victory the world has so long been waiting for. . . . true liberation, respect and concern . . FOR ALL.

And no matter what anyone says, Paul, never doubt for one moment that we can do it. . . . for it is my belief . . . out of the experience of a lifetime, that this is God's will, and that He is with us.

The foregoing is just a partial answer to the questions you have asked. It is my belief that God's presence has been made known to me by the four ways cited above.

Sincerely,

Lew Ayres

Joan Chandos Baez

Oct 15, 1980

Dear Paul,

    Thanks for your letter. I'll try and answer it.

    Yes, I believe in God — but he/she doesn't make himself/herself known to me in very obvious ways. It's more like a feeling of graciousness and happiness when I see something very beautiful — like a new baby in the arms of its mother, like a dark storm passing by and the sun coming out and warming my skin, like leaves covering the ground under a tree in the fall . . . God must have something to do with joy . . .

    and with sadness.

      and with kindness, beauty, & love

        but I don't claim to know,

yours,

Joan Baez

JOAN BAEZ
Folk singer, Founder—Resource Center for Nonviolence, Santa Cruz, CA
Author—*Daybreak*

PRESIDENT: PEARL BAILEY

P.O. BOX 52
NORTHRIDGE, CALIFORNIA 91328

November 12, 1976

Dear Paul:

Thank you for taking the time to write to me and for your interest in my belief in God for your survey.

You bet I believe in God! He has been very good to me and has blessed me with much — primarily the talent He gave me and the ability to meet, understand, love and care about all humanity. I have known Him all of my life — He has been a constant companion and the only true Physician.

I hope this gives you some idea of how strongly I believe in God and I hope your project will be a wonderful learning experience for you.

God bless you always and thank you again for having written to me.

All love,

Miss Pearl Bailey

PB/dw

PEARL BAILEY
Singer, actress—*Hello Dolly*

Rona Barrett

June 6, 1983

Mr. Paul Rifkin
674 Route 6A
East Sandwich, MA 02537

Dear Paul:

I most definitely do believe in a GOD . . . whether God looks like a person or is a force more powerful than anything we've yet to comprehend . . . my faith leads me to believe that such a power is out there in this vast universe.

My first encounter with "God" that I can recall occurred when I was five years old. I was born physically handicapped and a group of children one day followed me home from school and began taunting me with sticks. I fell to the sidewalk and prayed that someone would come along to help me up and protect me. Just then my best girlfriend arrived on the scene and literally dragged me into our apartment building. She saved me. Somehow I knew right there and then that somebody-up-there did not want me to be physically hurt more than I already was. From that moment on I began praying to "God" to help me. When I was a child I used to pray for very specific things and many times my prayers were answered.

In later years I discovered it is not necessary to pray for "specifics" but to ask God for "right direction" — and then what is meant for you shall be yours.

RONA BARRETT
Columnist

Writing such a short paragraph about one's belief in God is quite difficult. I hope, however, these few words will give you some idea of where I am coming from and my deep and abiding belief in "God."

May good thoughts...good days...and many of your wishes come true, Paul Rifkin.

Thank you for writing me.

Most sincerely yours,

Rona Barrett

ANNE BAXTER

Dear Paul Rifkin;

Young people think that "seeing is believing." But can you eat love like an ice cream cone? Can you wear it like a sweater?! No. But, it is visible in your parents' eyes. God is just as real. I've believed in him as long as I can remember praying before bedtime.

So many times in my life I've been desperate for more strength then I've had, and have prayed to God for that super-human strength. God has NEVER failed to give it. People often do. Try it. It works.

Sincerely,

Anne Baxt

ANNE BAXTER
Movie actress—*Ten Commandments*

September 22, 1980

Dear Paul Grifkin:

In reply to your letter of September 18 it is heartening to know of your selection of subject matter.

You have asked two questions: Do I believe in God. The answer is yes.

And how did he make himself known to me: The answer is from the beginning of my sense of realisation of all kinds of life, including my own, and the seasons and fruition of everything that grows in the fields and seas and forests and jungles and nests and cradles.

Its indisputable isn't it?

RALPH BELLAMY
Actor—*Rosemary's Baby*

Columbia Artists
Management Inc.

May 2, 1983

Mr. Paul Rifkin
674 Route 6A
East Sandwich, MA 02537

Dear Paul:

Yes, I do believe in God. He makes his presence known to me every morning when the sun rises and when life around me begins.

With best regards,

Sincerely,

Sir Rudolf Bing

SRB:CMD

SIR RUDOLPH BING
Manager—Metropolitan Opera, New York City

15

MEL BLANC

5-26-83

Dear Paul:

"Boruch Atow Adinoy"

Yes — I believe in God ever

since my "Briss" at the age of

ten days.

Mel Blanc

Copyright W.B.P.I.

MEL BLANC
Entertainer—voice of Bugs Bunny

VICTOR BORGE

Nov. 15/76

My dear Paul:

Yes, I believe that God is light and love, who made it possible for you to speak to me and me to you.

With kindest
regards,

Yours,

VICTOR BORGE
Comedian, pianist

THE DAVE BRUBECK QUARTET

221 MILLSTONE ROAD
WILTON, CONNECTICUT 06897
(203) 762-7710

December 17, 1982

Mr. Paul Rifkin
674 Rt. 6A
East Sandwich, MASS 02537

Dear Paul,

First of all, I would like to thank you for writing to me especially
requesting such a unique reply. My feelings are very strong about
God, and therefore I answer your first question of my belief with
a very firm yes.

God created the earth as he created all of us; His presence is
in the gift of Life.

Again, thank you Paul for your letter. Hopefully this will help
you in your school report. I wish you a very joyous holiday
season.

Sincerely,

Dave Brubeck

DAVE BRUBECK
Jazz musician, composer—"Beloved Son"

JOHN CAGE

101 WEST 18 STREET (5B) • NEW YORK, NEW YORK 10011

Paul Rifkin
RFD 2 opp Grant Rd
New Market, N.H. 03857

Oct. 7, 1980

I am not a member of a church. I studied the philosophy
of Zen Buddhism with Daisetz Suzuki in the late '40s.
We do not speak of God. We see each being whether
sentient or non-sentient as the Buddha. Creation has
no single center but is a multiplicity of centers in
interpenetration and non-obstruction. Nirvana (the goal)
is Samsara (this very moment and place).

With best wishes,

John Cage

JOHN CAGE
Composer, past president—Cunningham Dance Foundation
Author—*Mushroom Book, Empty Words*

August 4, 1983

Paul Rifkin
Grade 5
674 Rt. 6A
East Sandwich
MASS 02537

Dear Paul:

Yes, I believe in God and His presence is constantly around you in birds, trees, animals—yes, animals from ants to elephants.

God is life.

Sincerely,

Frank Capra

FRANK CAPRA
Motion picture producer and director—*It Happened One Night,*
Pocketful of Miracles, Lost Horizon

Dear Paul,

About your school paper— I was trying to get to sleep at about 11:00 in the morning and I was in such a state that I started thinking—what if there was no earth, no sky, no anything?! Even to the point that I visualized everything including myself no bigger than the head of a pin. At that point I cried out aloud for God's help— and it was there that I realized that I truly believed in him.

Good luck,

Hoagy Carmichael

Hoagy Carmichael

HOAGY CARMICHAEL
Composer, actor—"Stardust," "Georgia on My Mind"

HARRY CHAPIN

January 17, 1977

Paul Rifkin
4212 25th St.
San Francisco, CA 94114

Dear Paul,

In response to your letter the following is a poem from
my poetry book, <u>Looking...Seeing.</u>

"An Admission"

Being modern
and agnosticated
I don't possess a God
to push and pull about
to match fate's idle motions.

But every once and a while,
not very often
let me add quickly,
being only human
I am prone to feeling
lost and somewhat miniscule.
Shyly I place
some sort of Being,
entirely nonreligious
let me assure you,
above me in the firmament.

I let Him laugh
at my endeavors
and grant myself,
only at these weakened moments
the grace of Someone
Else's recognition
of my very doubtful
existence.

I hope this answers your question.

Sincerely,

Harry Chapin

HC/dr

HARRY CHAPIN
Singer, songwriter

Dear Paul,

You asked if I believe in God. Well, I believe that the Universe, Nature, Life, in all its million forms is sacred. And that it is all God— as are each one of us. Each one of us is a miracle, and we are related to all the other billions and billions of miracles in the world whether it be a speck of intergallactic dust, one of the few remaining red kites, an endangered whale, or an atom. So, to me, the idea of splitting an atom is a crime. And making nuclear weapons which can destroy this sacred planet, is an equal crime.

But I don't believe in a white God with a long beard sitting in the clouds, turning a blind eye to all these crimes.

First of all, why should God be a man? It seems really silly that it should be a man, or a woman, but men are so war like, I think God would be more likely to be a woman if it was anything.

No, I think we all have Godliness within us. It's just a question of not losing it when all we are encouraged to do is think of <u>things</u> & <u>getting</u> things, & making money, which is the opposite of God, because that encourages Greed. Anyway, I wish you luck with your survey, Take care,

I wish you a happy life —

Julie Christie,

JULIE CHRISTIE
Movie actress—*Dr. Zhivago, McCabe and Mrs. Miller*

CBS
NEWS

A Division of CBS Inc.
524 West 57 Street
New York, New York 10019
(212) 975-4321

23 March 1983

Dear Mr. Rifkin:

I suppose I do believe in God. At least I believe that there is a guiding power in the Universe, usually benign. Having been brought up in a religious family, I tend to call that God, but I think that personalizes Him too much. I cannot visualize Him at all and think of his influence as a force, a power, rather than as someone in whose image I was created. I haven't the faintest notion whether we look alike or not.

I have had no revelatory experience and couldn't tell you how God made his presence known to me. It is something I have grown up with and I sense his presence in all things, however contradictory it may sometime appear to me.

Yours sincerely,

Charles Collingwood

CHARLES COLLINGWOOD
Radio and TV commentator

MICHAEL CRICHTON

December 9, 1976

Dear Paul Rifkin:

Thank you for your letter. I do believe in God, although I am not sure I can make my beliefs clear. (They aren't clear to me.) I have come to my beliefs through my understanding of science, particularly physics, which is ordinarily thought to be Godless, but isn't.

I do not have much interest in organized religion. Organized religion is a business and nothing else, unless you want to think of it as a way to organize wars efficiently. Also, organized religion tells you what to think, and I believe the only way to know about God is to find out on your own. What somebody else tells you is of very little use except on an ethical or moral level. But ethics and morals are just arbitrary social agreements, no matter what anybody tells you.

I believe that we are all God, and God is all of us. But this means you can find out everything you need to know by yourself, by what you see and what you feel. Nobody knows any more than you do—even though you're just in the fifth grade.

Best wishes,

Michael Crichton

MICHAEL CRICHTON
Author of *Andromeda Strain*

Bing Crosby

November 8, 1976

Dear Paul:

Yes, I certainly do believe in God. I have since
my first conscious moment in this life, and of
course, I went to a Jesuit school for eight years,
which only fortified my beliefs.

God has never made his presence known to me, but I
only have to look around me to know that he exists.
How else can you explain the world we see around
us in all its wonders?

Only the existence of a Divine Creator could have
made it possible.

I hope this proves suitable for you, Paul –

All best wishes for the success of your project,

Bing Crosby

BC:lm

Mr. Paul Rifkin
Grade 5
4212 25th Street
San Francisco, California 94114

BING CROSBY
Crooner, movie star

yes i Do Love
God and have
All ways Love God

Love You

BO DIDDLEY
Rock and roll musician

PHYLLIS DILLER

August 10, 1983

Dear Paul

Thank you for your nice letter. Here is my answer to your question, "DO YOU BELIEVE IN GOD?"

> "I believe in the spirit of good, the life force, nature. That is my "form" of what some people call God. I cannot picture a man in human form as God."

Good luck with your project!

Best wishes

Phyllis Diller

Phyllis Diller

PHYLLIS DILLER
Comedienne

HUGH DOWNS

November 5, 1976

Paul Rifkin
Grade 5
4212 25th Street
San Francisco, California 94114

Dear Paul:

Thank you for your letter with the question "Do you believe in God?" which I will try to answer:

The answer is yes. But it is important to explain in what way I believe. For many people it is comforting to accept a specific dogma and descriptions of God drawn largely by other people living and dead. I find it is not possible for me to accept any of these sets of descriptions as a package. While I respect the right of other people to accept formal religions and I respect their sincere beliefs, I do not personally believe in the way of any other people I have met or read about. This means that I am like a man named Carlyle who once said "There is one true church of which at present I am the only member."

For years I thought I would find proof of the existence of God through scientific and logical truths. I have come to believe that any such "proofs" would limit the concept of God and a limited God is not what I believe in. His presence was made known to me on a personal level that has nothing to do with scientific proofs one way or the other. Since this is very complicated I probably could not describe it to you without the danger of limiting the concept and defeating my purpose.

HUGH DOWNS
Radio and TV broadcaster— *"Home Show," "Today Show," "Over Easy"*

Perhaps I could throw some light on it by explaining some things that God is _not_, in my belief. He is not a statue or idol, or a kindly old gentleman with a beard looking down from somewhere above the clouds, nor anything totally outside myself (and yourself.)

He is not a symbol used by temporal powers and organizations to make me behave. He is not a product of my fears and hopes nor a result of my intellectual deliberations.

I have only glimpses of something totally indescribable. Anyone determined to know God fully must probably be prepared to make enormous sacrifices in specific desires and ego ("He who would save his life must lose it.")

I am coming more and more to believe that no harm can come to a good man in life or death. This was said first over 2,000 years ago by a man named Socrates in Greece. I hope that you are aiming at becoming a good man. You will probably develop your own way of arriving at a faith, but becoming a good man is one way.

Best wishes to you.

Sincerely,

Hugh Downs

HD:jf

CBS
NEWS

A Division of CBS Inc.
524 West 57 Street
New York, New York 10019
(212) 975-4321

Dear Paul,

Please forgive the delay in answering your letter. I have been away on vacation, followed by hospitalization and recuperation for an appendectomy. I do hope my answer is not too late for your report.

Yes, I do indeed believe in God. He made his presence known to me from my very earliest days of understanding, through attending Sunday School, joining the church, and on a day-to-day basis in the general observation of nature and its wonders — the birth of a baby, the change of seasons, the migration of birds, the precision of the sunrise and sunset, the wonders of the heavens and the deep-rooted belief that all of these marvels were the work of His creation. His presence has also been manifested to me many times in the answering of prayer.

Good luck with your report, and please let me know how you made out on it.

Sincerely,

Douglas Edwards

Master Paul Rifkin
674 Rt. 6A
East Sandwich, Massachusetts 02537

March 10, 1983

DOUGLAS EDWARDS
Radio and TV news reporter

Master Paul Rifkin
674 Route 6-A
East Sandwich, Massachusetts 02537

Dear Paul:

Sure, I believe in God. I have ever since I was five years old and my mother and I were driving through one of those outrageous hail storms in a buggy pulled by a chestnut mare. The hail finally got so intense, the mare raised up on its hind legs, and I thought she was coming right back over on us. My mother said, "Don't worry son; God will take care of us."

Holding onto the reins with one hand, and reaching for the buggy whip with the other, she brought that whip down over that mare's back so hard the mare straightened out and never stopped running with us until we reached our homestead.

I wondered for awhile if God were associated with a buggy whip, but I certainly knew from then on, there had to be a God.

Sincerely,

Ralph Edwards

RALPH EDWARDS
TV and radio producer, Master of ceremonies and creator of "This Is Your Life"
Creator and producer of "Name That Tune"

August 18th, 1983

Dear Paul:

Thank you for your nice letter, and I am so glad you asked me these questions. Yes, I do believe in God and in His Son, Jesus Christ. I believe the founding fathers of our country knew the wisdom of putting God in charge of our country and each of us need to put Him in charge of our lives — every aspect of it.

God has been a very real and personal friend to me. He has richly blessed my life from the time I was 18 years old and turned to Him for help. He was there, and I'll never forget it.

Good luck and God Bless.

Rhonda Fleming

RHONDA FLEMING
Movie actress, singer—*Spellbound, Gunfight at the O.K. Corral*

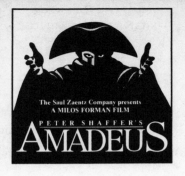

The Saul Zaentz Company presents
A MILOS FORMAN FILM
PETER SHAFFER'S
AMADEUS

Dear Paul,

Yes I believe in God. Not necessarily in the image of the old man with long white beard, but I do believe in a divine creator spirit.

I just can not accept an idea that nature in its incredible complexity and the Life itself happened by accident.

Yours,

MILOS FORMAN
Film director—*One Flew Over the Cuckoo's Nest, Hair, Amadeus*

Dear Paul Rifkin,

Of course there is a
God—He made His presence
known to me when I married
one of His Angels—my wife!—

Sincerely

Martin Gabel

Nov 7, 76

Dear Paul,

    Yes. I believe in a God . . .
    He made his presence known to me through the birth of my beautiful child.

        Sincerely,

zsa zsa

ZSA ZSA GABOR
Actress—*Lili, Moulin Rouge*

Dear Paul

In answer to your question (Do you Believe in God?) yes I do believe in <u>God</u>, but better still, Let me go one step further and say i not only believe in God, but I believe <u>God</u>. You said in your letter describe how God made his presence known to you. Well,, I surrendered my will to his will. Which means I realized that I could not save myself. therefore I must have someone to save me. Let me try to Explain. at the ocean we are allowed to go into the water at any public beach. to provide a margin of safety they always have Life guards Present. they are there to come to everybody's assistance, when they should call for help, help would be provided. You don't have to pay for this help in order to be saved from drowning. You need simply to call out for help in the water and the Life guards who have been given the authority to rescue you will do so without payment because it has already been payd for by the city government. When God made his presence known to me I realized that it is by grace we are saved—not by works or payment or any other acts of our will. We simply have to want to be saved and then cry out for him to save us (the Lord God). Jesus was the final payment provided by God so that we need not have to pay for our salvation. All we need to do is cry out for God to forgive us of our sins and save us. And just as the illustration of the Life Guard's, this act of grace is given. I hope this helps you. God Bless you.

Sincerely in Jesus' name

(Little) Anthony Gourdine.

"LITTLE ANTHONY" GOURDINE
Rock and roll performer, of Little Anthony & the Imperials—"Tears on My Pillow"

CAPPY PRODUCTIONS INC.

October 14, 1980

Paul Rifkin
67Y Route 6A
East Sandwich, MA 02537

Dearl Paul:

Thank you for your letter.

To answer your question, my belief in God stems from an incident that changed my parents' lives, and in turn, my life.

My older sister Judith was dying, with no hope of recovery. The doctors who were treating her gave up hope, and told my parents that there was nothing more they could do for her. She was beyond medical help.

My father, who was not a religious man, went to the synagogue and prayed for Judith's life. He prayed that if God spared her he would become a devout Jew.

He spent a half-hour in the synagogue, and upon his return home, he saw smiles on the faces of Judith's doctors. They greeted my father with the news that something miraculous had happened in the last half-hour, and that for the first time in weeks Judith was responding to treatment.

Judith recovered and is alive, happy, and healthy, living in Florida. From the day of her recovery, the belief in God has been part of our lives.

Sincerely,

Bud Greenspan

BG/das

BUD GREENSPAN
Film company executive *The Olympiad*

monty hall

November 17, 1976

Dear Paul,

Thank you for asking me to give my opinion on your question "Do you believe in God?"—although I am not quite sure that my answer will be enlightening.

I suppose that when one looks at the universe and how all the plants are held in some kind of supernatural control and how even the gift of life is a miracle; and that when one studies all the elements of wind, water, fire—then one has to believe that there is something bigger than all of us mortals who inhabit this planet, and indeed all planets.

Yet it is so difficult for me sometimes to accept the fact that there is a benevolent deity when little children I have known and loved die before they have even known a full life, when so much havoc is spread throughout the world by famine, by war, by flood. To have someone tell us this is God's way is an easy answer, but not for me. I have wrestled with this question all my life.

I suppose the answer is for all of us to believe that there is something of God in each one of us: the way we conduct our lives, the way we treat our fellow men. This is as much as I can offer you. The rest is up to the teachers.

You ask if God has made his presence known to me, and I am afraid I cannot answer in the affirmative; but if you ask if there is something divine about the birth of a child who grows up in your image, then I can answer honestly—yes, that I have experienced.

I congratulate you for making this survey; and while the answers that you receive will differ, I am sure, it is something for you and your schoolmates to think about now and for years to come.

My kind wishes to you,

MONTY HALL
TV producer, actor, host on *Let's Make a Deal*

MARVIN HAMLISCH

Paul Rifkin
Grade 5
674 Rt. 6A
East Sandwich
Massachusetts 02537

Dear Paul:

I certainly do believe in G-d.

However, I do not necessarily think that it is important if He has made His presence known to me, but just the opposite— that is, if I have made my presence known to Him. Through my deeds and actions in trying to be a good human being, I believe I make my presence known to Him. And it is precisely because I feel that way, that I do not have to seek out G-d, all I have to do is know that He is there, watching over me.

Sincerely,

Marvin Hamlisch

MARVIN HAMLISCH
Composer—*A Chorus Line* (Broadway musical)

Doug Henning Magic

May 13, 1983

PAUL RIFKIN
674 Rt 6A
East Sandwich, MA 02537

Dear Paul,

Thank you very much for your letter. I've asked Doug your question, "Do you believe in God?" and this is what he said.

"Yes, I believe in God. He is within me, and everyone, and all things. I practice Transcendental Meditation which takes me deep within my own self where I feel very close to God."

I hope this helps you out with your report. I have enclosed a picture of Doug to include with your project.

Magically yours,

Debbie Kirsner
Secretary to Doug Henning

/dk
enc.

DOUG HENNING
Illusionist; co-creator, star, rock magic musical *The Magic Show*

Aug 17, 1983

Dear Paul

I am answering your questions at the request of my husband.

1. Yes Burl believes in God!

2. God made His Presence known to a young Illinois Boy through the grace of a loving family. Through the joy of natures renewal and when he heard and recognized his own heart beat—he knew he was of God—God Bless You.

Yours in Light

Dorthy
Mrs Burl Ives

CAVELIGHT MUSIC

Dear Paul,

I don't usually answer the personal mail as it mostly consists of people asking for autographs and other silly things like that. However, your project interests me and I wonder if you could send me a copy of it when it's finished. If so, send it to the above address.

Now to your question: Hopefully you won't mind a longer answer than "yes" or "no". I have faith in the spirit that animates us, and I believe that to be close to God is to work as little against this spirit as possible I also believe that to do this a human being must first work to become Conscious (in other words, on the average we are asleep and we must wake up) and to stay Conscious in order to participate in the Spirit (or to work with God) When we are conscious, then it becomes obvious what to <u>do</u> (then you don't <u>believe</u> in God, really, you <u>know</u> God).

So, this means that the second part of your question is also a little tricky. God did not make his presence known to me. I've tried to work to discover his presence in me. This is what I think we are here for. You see, God's already done his work and is present, so we must work hard to be <u>Conscious</u> of <u>Him</u>. That is how He is known Then, however, there are not two things (God and you or God and me), there is only God.

I hope this isn't too complicated as I am really not a writer, but again I really appreciate your letter. I have a son in fifth grade and I would only hope that his class reports were as valuable to him.

Sincerely,

KEITH JARRETT
P.O. Box 127
Oxford, N.J. 07863

KEITH JARRETT
Jazz pianist

September 26, 1983

Paul Rifkin
674 Route 6A
East Sandwich, MA. 02537

Dear Paul,

     Your letter finally reached me last week, and I apologize for this delayed reply. Yes, Paul, I definitely believe in God.

     Darwin's theory of <u>Natural Selection</u> may have something to do with a definition of how life has evolved, and the "Big Bang" concept of the origin of the Universe may also have something to do with it...but only a God could be capable of such astonishing miracles.

     My very best wishes to you for success and happiness, and thank you for your letter.

Sincerely yours,

Stacy Keach

STACY KEACH
Actor, director—*The Life of Christ, Butterfly*

Spain.

May 3rd. 1983.

Dear Paul,

In answer to your question: 'Do you believe in God', the answer is of course 'Yes'. But there are many, many ways of believing in God as we know all too well. I do not believe in God in the sentimental form of the white-robed, golden-haired <u>human</u>, as illustrated in many books and bibles. I <u>do</u> believe in an infinite <u>MIND</u>, and its infinite manifestation. God is all in all, and is in us and around us at all times. We have only to call on this power and <u>believe</u>. In this sense His presence has made itself known to me by showing me the way when one is beset with problems and decisions.

I hope this answer to your question, (which is a very difficult one in these troubled times) will satisfy you.

With all best wishes,

<u>Deborah Kerr.</u>

Paul Rifkin,
Grade 5, 67Y RT 6A,
East Sandwich,
Mass. 02537,
<u>*U.S.A.*</u>

Walter Lantz
PRODUCTIONS, INC.

Dear Paul

In answer to your letter, If I believe in God? Yes I do, very much.

I was an Alter Boy when I was your age, and we were taught what belief in God meant.

If the young people of this generation had more respect for their elders and believed in God, maybe, we wouldn't have so much crime.

Sincerely

Walter Lantz

WALTER LANTZ
Animated cartoon producer, Creator—Woody Woodpecker

Janet Leigh Brandt

August 23, 1983

Mr. Paul Rifkin
674 Rt 6A
East Sandwich
Mass. 02537

Dear Paul,

Yes, I do believe in God. I see Him in every delicate leaf, in every massive tree, in an exquisite snow flake, in each blade of grass. I see Him in the balance of life He created, from an ant to an elephant.

I see Him in all good.

Sincerely,

Janet Leigh

JANET LEIGH
Movie actress—*Angels in the Outfield, Psycho*

COURTYARD FILMS LTD

29th April, 1983

Paul Rifkin, Esq.,
Grade 5,
674 RT 6A,
East Sandwich,
Mass. 02537,
U.S.A.

Dear Paul Rifkin,

Thank you for your letter.

The answer to your question is:
NO I DO NOT AND NEVER HAVE BELIEVED
IN THE EXISTENCE OF A GOD.

I wish you every success with your class
project.

Best wishes,

Yours sincerely,

Richard Lester.

RICHARD LESTER
Film director—*A Hard Day's Night, Help, Superman II*

4/19/83

Dear Paul:

Yes, I believe in God.

How did He make his presence known to me? Whenever I look up at the stars or sail across a mighty ocean I feel his presence.

Best wishes,

[signature: Art]

ART LINKLETTER
Radio and TV broadcaster—"People Are Funny"
Author—*Kids Say the Darndest Things*

4/5.

Dear Paul.

I would like to help you but I think it is too personal a matter to discuss with someone I do not know.

Your,

Robert MacNeil

ROBERT MacNEIL
THE MACNEIL-LEHRER REPORT

ROBERT MacNEIL
Broadcast journalist—*The MacNeil/Lehrer Report*

Dear Paul Rifkin————

Yes! I believe in God!
He believes in me————. The least I can do is believe
in him.

Have a god believing summer.

Karl Malden

KARL MALDEN
Actor—*A Streetcar Named Desire, On the Waterfront, Streets of San Francisco*

COMPAGNIE DE MIME
MARCEL
MARCEAU

Paris,
March 9th 1983

Dear Paul,

It is a very hard question to answer: "Do you believe in God ?"

I do not believe especially in one God, but in a superior being which could be the secret of the creation of the Universe.

I believe in the Godly and in the Divine in the spirit of Man which is the inspiration guiding humanity. In this sense I believe in God.

God has his presence in me through my heart, through the love I share with humanity and through my inspiration I hope to preserve for a long time to create and always bring out the best of my own self from me for the rest of my life.

With my best wishes, always your

BIP

Marcel MARCEAU

Excuse, please, the correction of that letter. I hope it is alright like this.

Tonight Show   NBC Television Network Division
National Broadcasting Company, Inc.

October 26, 1980

Paul Rifkin
674 Rt. 6 A
E. Sandwich, MA 02537

Dear Paul:

Hope my answer to your letter for a class report is not too
late. Your letter came to my office while I was away and I
have just returned.

Yes, I do believe in God. God made his presence known to
me during the Korean War. My best friend and I took turns
flying. We both went on leave together and when we returned
I went out on the first hop, my buddy took the second hop.
When I went to relieve him I found he had been killed. I
knew then God was watching over me.

Hope the above answers your questions adequately for your
report.

Thank you for your interest.

Cordially,

Ed McMahon

ED McMAHON
TV announcer—"The Tonight Show"

September 8, 1983

Mr. Paul Rifkin
Grade 5
674 Rt. 6A
East Sandwich, Massachusetts 02537

Dear Paul:

Of course I believe in God. I don't know how anyone could get through life without a firm belief and faith in the goodness of God. There is no problem that we encounter on this earth too big for God to solve for us if we turn our difficulties over to Him in prayer. We also must always remember to thank God everyday for all our blessings. We can pray to Him at any hour of the day. We don't have to wait until we are going to bed at night to talk to Him, and the more you pray, the closer you will feel His presence. If I have a problem, anytime I ask God for guidance, the answer always comes, and it is always right.

We seem to work hard at everything we do, such as in your case, going to school, doing your homework and playing in sports, but we never give the same amount of time to God.

If you make God part of your life as the best friend you will ever have in this world, you will have a fruitful, successful life.

With every good wish to you always.

Sincerely,

Audrey Meadows

AUDREY MEADOWS
Actress—lead role in "The Honeymooners," "The Jackie Gleason Show"

Jayne Meadows

Twenty-Ninth
November
1 9 8 3

Mr. Paul Rifkin
674 Route 6A
East Sandwich, MA 02537

Dear Mr. Rifkin:

The following is a slightly revised version of the statement
sent to you some time ago:

> It appears to me that God makes his presence
> known in the world of nature that lies all about us,
> from the morning sun to the stars and moon, from
> the trees and flowers, the wind, life-giving rain, the
> animal creatures of the earth, family, relatives, friends
> and fellow workers, from the food and drink the earth
> provides—they all seem to me to be gifts from the
> creator, including the gifts of health, talent, the joys—
> even the sorrow of life, and the final one—are, I feel,
> ordained by God.
> Also, I experienced a few years ago a dramatic
> healing that may have had miraculous aspects. In any
> event, I am grateful to God for life itself.

Love,

Jayne Meadows Allen

JMA:jla

JAYNE MEADOWS
Actress, Movies—*David and Bathsheba*

Dear Paul,

This is Mrs. Montoya writing. You probably know that my husband is from Spain; he doesn't write english, so he has asked me to answer.

Yes, he definitely believes in God. He was brought up in a religious family and never doubted that there was a God. After he grew up and thought more about it, he felt inside himself that there must be a power greater than all of us. He believes there is a God of all the human race not just the Christians or the Jews. Also, he feels closer to God in the country than in church.

I hope you will do well with your survey.

Good luck!

Sally Montoya

Dear Paul:
     Yes! I do believe in God!
*and those who don't are <u>stupid</u>! Observe the Miracles of Creation
that Surround you . . . the Starry heavens, the vast, restless ocean,
the mighty mountains the sun—the moon—change of seasons—flowers
in the spring etc. etc. . Can any one believe they all happened by
accident or by chance?*
     *I have always been a religious person from my early years.
My Mother taught me how to pray and believe. She taught me to
see myself as a child of God—that He created me and cares about
me. I am a Roman Catholic.*
     *I keep praying for more faith and love—I get this through
the Bible—going to daily Mass, praying the Rosary, being charitable
and always conscious of Gods presence. Abiding by the 10
Commandments—and trying to live the <u>Good life</u> for the Kingdom
of Heaven.*
     *I hope this information is satisfactory Paul.—
God Bless You and I hope this letter has helped <u>you</u> <u>too</u>!!*

Love

HILDEGARDE NEFF
Actress, chanteuse

57

October 14, 1980

425 Lafayette Street
New York, New York 10003
212 598-7100
Cable NEWSHAKES

NEW YORK SHAKESPEARE FESTIVAL

Joseph Papp Producer

Mr. Paul Rifkin
674 Route 6A
East Sandwich, MA   02537

Dear Paul:

When I was your age, God was to be found in the synagogue, a small storefront shul in Brooklyn. He was everywhere: in my father's "talis" (prayer shawl), in his tefilin (philactories) that appeared on my father's arm and forehead every morning, in the cracked voice of the neighborhood cantor who was a glazier by trade, in the chanting of the small, poor devoted congregation, but most of all I saw God in the arc which housed the precious Torahs, the scrolls covered with soft velvet material and decorated in "gold thread" with the great lion of Judah. When these huge scrolls were lifted high into the air, I held my breath. "If a Torah is dropped," my father would say, "it would be a tragedy of immense proportions. We would have to fast for forty days and nights to compensate." In the torahs, to me, lay the secrets of the universe. Here God's breath permeates the elegant Hebrew letters covering the strong parchment. But God's presence was everywhere in my life, especially on the Sabbath eve and during the high holy days. When the ram's horn (Shofar) was sounded at the close of Yom Kippur (day of atonement), it was God's voice I heard forgiving us all for our sins. Today I still find God in shul and in the memory of my parents, plain and simple Jewish folk who gave me an everlasting gift of cultural continuity.

Paul, I hope these words will help you in your report and perhaps in your life.

Sincerely,

JP/tc

JOSEPH PAPP
Theatrical director, producer—New York Shakespeare Festival

EMI STUDIOS
BOREHAMWOOD
HERTFORDSHIRE

December 14th 1976

Mr. Paul Rifkin
4212 25th Street
San Francisco, 94114

Dear Paul:

In answer to your letter of October 30th: —yes.

One morning in Sausalito when the fog broke, and I was not hungover, and one night in Malibu when I recognized what the speed of light was.

Sincerely,

SAM PECKINPAH

SAM PECKINPAH
Motion picture director—*The Wild Bunch, Straw Dogs*

JOHN RITTER

Dear Paul—

    <u>Yes</u> I do believe in God. And HE has
comforted me all my life with His love and Spirit—

Best Always—

John Ritter [signature]

JOAN RIVERS

November 1983

Dear Paul,

Yes, I believe in God and he has made his presence known to me by giving me a beautiful daughter, a good life and the ability to make people happy.

Much happiness and good luck to you always.

Most sincerely,

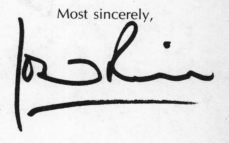

CBS
NEWS

A Division of CBS Inc.
524 West 57 Street
New York. New York 10019
(212) 975-4321

Dear Paul,

No, of course I dont and anyone who tells you that there is a god who made his or her presence known to him or her is hallucinating or not telling the truth.

ANDREW ROONEY
Writer, TV analyst—*60 Minutes*

MARK RUSSELL
office
2800 Wisconsin Ave., N.W. Suite 810
Washington, D.C. 20007
202/362-5045

November 2, 1983

Mr. Paul Rifkin
THE GOD LETTERS
674 Route 6-A
East Sandwich, MA 02537

Dear Mr. Rifkin,

I am delighted to enclose permission for Mark's contribution to your book.

I cannot resist adding my own and hope it will be included. You have my permission to use it and I will even buy a copy.

AND GOD CREATED THE WORLD IN SIX DAYS
AND ON THE SEVENTH DAY
SHE CLEANED HEAVEN

Sincerely yours,

Linda Ruskin

Linda Ruskin
Assistant to Mr. Russell

LINDA RUSKIN
Assistant to Mark Russell

April 19, 1983

Master Paul Rifkin
674 Route 6A
East Sandwich, Mass 02537

Dear Paul,

Thank you for asking me to participate in your fifth grade class report. My answer to your question is, "yes, I believe in God, because I have seen more than 18,250 sunrises and every one of them has been exactly on time."

Sincerely,

Mark Russell

Mark Russell

June 8, 1983

Dear Paul:

Yes, I believe in God. In fact, praying and meditating on God's Presence in my life is most important to me. I first felt the presence of the Lord in my heart like the cool sensation of a baby's trembling sigh. When I heard a soulful and glorious speech of Martin Luther King, Jr., I understood dedication to God and felt His call in my life.

I pray He is real to you, too.

God Bless you,

Carlos Santana

CARLOS SANTANA
Musician—Leader of Santana

Dear Paul—I could answer your question yes or no, and in either case, it would be meaningless without a long discussion of what you mean by the words "believe" or "God". I urge you to pay less attention to what people say, and more to what people do

Sincerely

平
和

PETE SEEGER
Folk singer, Composer

July - 8, 83

Paul,

Thanks for your letter. Starting right off, yes I do believe in God. I found the God of my understanding in a hospital in Los Angeles about 5½ years ago while I was recovering from a problem with drinking. I found out that I had a disease called alcoholism & so far to this day I haven't had a drink or pill I wouldn't be alive today if I wouldn't have found God. I hope you have him in your life.

Have a good year in school—

all the best!

Del Shannon

DEL SHANNON
Rock and roll performer

Dear Paul,

Thank you for your letter—
In answer to your question — Yes I do believe in God!
He has made his presence known to me in every living thing I have ever felt—

Sincerely,

7/24/83

Kay Starr

'8/14/'83

Dear Paul Rifkin;

Do I believe in GOD? Usually this is such a personal matter that one does not discuss it with a stranger, but I feel our belief in Him should keep all people from being strangers.

I think first I must tell you that I am ¾ American Indian. Therefore I see the Maker in all things. All His signs are all about us. All his creatures are of his making. It escapes me how anyone who is in full custody of all their senses does not stop and wonder about it all.

Since I am a singer I feel <u>that</u> is a gift from GOD. I thank him constantly for the joy it gives me to perform as well as the enjoyment it gives to some people. This is my way of reaching people without having arms long enough to actually touch them. It would be hard to explain this feeling to a grownup, perhaps you will understand.

I must compliment your instructor upon the courage it must take to make this subject a lesson and my hat comes off to you Sir, for having the spirit to ask people of my profession. I hope you will not be disappointed in the response.

If everyone will just believe in "something", perhaps that will be our Salvation.

Good luck with your life,
and your school project

Kay Starr

KAY STARR
Singer

Dear friend,

Thank you for your letter, and for showing your appreciation for my music.

I'm sure you will find that hidden inside my music was the soul of a seeker, and I am now happy to say that I have found what I was looking for.

I was given the Holy Qur'an in 75 and since then I have not looked back. The Qur'an is the last message sent for the guidance of mankind and it will remain so up to the Last Day when all things will be known. After reading it I decided to embrace Islam and worship Allah, Lord of the Universe, Creator of life and death, and to seek true knowledge of Him

May Allah guide you to the straight path, there is no god but God, and Muhammad is His servant and messenger.

CAT STEVENS (YUSUF ISLAM)
Singer, musician, composer

loretta Swit

14 August 1983

Dear Paul,

I will try and assist you with your school project:

My sense of "believing in God" is that I feel there is within each of us a part of the total universe. All living creatures are related one to the other. We share time and space integrally. We all together comprise the universal spirit—and it is for each of us to enhance that core of the spirit which is uniquely ours that we might contribute to the goodness of the universe in our own personal way.

I wish you hapiness in your life.

Sincerely,

LORETTA SWIT
/r

LORETTA SWIT
Actress—"M*A*S*H"

To Paul Ryskin—

Dear Paul—
    I do believe
in God.

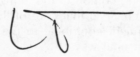

LILY TOMLIN
Comedienne, actress

Dear Paul Rifkin,

It took a while for your letter to reach me, so probably time is out already long ago for your class report. But I will give you my answer anyway.

I do believe in God. Why I do is much more difficult to tell in a few words. However, in spite of all the tragedies to mankind, big ones and small ones, that are happening all the time, I can still not find any reason to think that He does not exist. A great Swedish poet once wrote, that although we cannot see God in person- or a god- or any gods- we continuously see this influence. He is here with us all the time, but he is disguised. "If a look bid us mingle in quiet Agape- us, dull and coldly single as most men be; if a hand, all unbidden, like true celestial balm on soul misery-ridden, should touch our palm; and if a radiance guide us, where we tormented trod- then unrevealed beside us there walks a god." (Hjalmar Gullberg).

All good wishes.

Max Von Sydow

MAX VON SYDOW
Actor—*The Exorcist*

73

July 25, 1983

Paul Rifkin
674, Rte. 6A
East Sandwich, MA 02537

Dear Paul,

Do I believe in God? A very definite yes!

There have been three occasions in my life when I quite honestly didn't think I could handle it. Each time I stood very, very still and simply thought "Help Me" with every ounce of my strength. In all three instances the strength to take one step forward at a time came from somewhere—from Someone.

The important thing to remember to do is—on the <u>good</u> days as well as all the days in between—be still for a moment and say "Thank You."

Good luck on your project, Paul, and thanks for your letter.

Sincerely,

Betty

Betty

BW/gc

BETTY WHITE
Actress, comedienne—*The Mary Tyler Moore Show*

Dear Paul,

Thanks for your letter.

I'm not sure about God, but I believe there is definitely a power that governs us.

I believe this because of the way nature recycles itself. And I believe that some power designed the human body as an almost perfect machine.

I believe that we will never understand or know about God (or whatever power)—just as hundreds of years ago man could never understand how we can transfer pictures and words around the world, live. And if man has this power now, then there are even greater powers out there that we will probably never learn. At least not in this life.

Meanwhile, enjoy it, and good luck

Fred Willard

FRED WILLARD
Actor—*Fernwood 2 Night, Real People*

Memo From

Dear Paul Rifkin

It is not possible to answer your letter accurately because you fail to mention which God?

> The Hebrew God
> The Christian God
> The Islam God
> The Hindu God
> > or any other?

Good Health always

Dr. Paul Winchell

Dr. Paul Winchell

PAUL WINCHELL
Actor, ventriloquist

Joel-Peter Witkin

New Mexico   April 10, 1983

Dear Paul,

Your letter is of great interest to me. Yes, I believe in God. I
see Him in all things; in the life of my son, the love of my wife,
in my work; in things humble and grand. His presence was
known again to me in the love your parents have for you in
the raising of such a fine young man. Creation did not stop on
the end of the sixth day, it continues through us, through all
time.

Fame is simply a name, an action, a life known to many. I
may be known for reasons good or bad. Respect, however can
only be felt in love, when the human spirit grows to feel, to
sense higher states of selfless giving.

When I was a child I had a hero. He wasn't famous. He was
an old cripple man who I saw every morning passing my house
on his way to church. I never saw his face because he was too
bent over in his slow agony; in his pain he dragged himself along
the fences and walls of the buildings. He was always dressed
in a pin-striped suit and wore a large black hat. At times I could
hear through his moaning words in Italian- prayers. One
morning I found myself having a great need to go to church. I
went on Sundays with my mother but that day I <u>had to</u> go,
something, some great needful purpose compelled me. I sat alone
in silence for a time praying and then admiring the paintings
and sculptures. Then a bell rang. It was the beginning of the
Mass. I participated in the service and when it came time for
Holy Communion I walked to the altar and knelt down. I was
so engrossed in the service and the expectation of receiving
Christ into my soul and body in Communion that I hadn't noticed
the sound next to me. It came from the old cripple man I saw
every morning. He was kneeling next to me at the altar on my
right side. I then saw his fine thin hands outstretched to hold
the Host. Then I heard again his praying. But most of all I could

JOEL-PETER WITKIN
Photographer

77

see his face. It was radiant. Such a face I'd only seen in paintings and sculpture in church and museums. I sat in silence after the Mass was over knowing I had seen and felt the courage and love that old crippled man had for God and all things.

I never saw the old man after that day. I was told soon after that he had died. I could only wonder about the history of his life and all the people and things he had known and loved. Beauty can be found in all things because the presence of God exists.

Yours In Light,

Joel-Peter Witkin

Joel-Peter Witkin,
servant of God

July 8, 1983

Mr. Paul Rifkin
5th Grade
674 Rt. 6-A
East Sandwich, MA 02537

My dear Paul:

YES, I BELIEVE IN GOD! I do not necessarily see Him
with a beard, sitting on top of a cloud, however, in my
67 years on this earth He has come to me when I needed
Him, on many occasions. I can best describe this as
follows. When I have needed that extra push, physically
or mentally, I call for His help in my own way, and I
am most humbly greatful to Him for the number of times
He has helped me.

Paul, I hope this answers your question. It is the only
answer I have.

From Me to You—

[signature]

KEENAN WYNN
Movie actor

PIA

Dear Paul,

I've been touring and just got your letter—I'm sorry if it delayed your project but here's my answer to your question.

I discovered God on my first Christmas and now I realize he's in everything we do, everyday of our lives. Without Him we wouldn't be here. He watches over us. He's someone greater than we are and is responsible for the beauty of nature and people. Besides, God is love.

Good luck with your project. All the best,

Pia Zadora

PIA ZADORA
Actress—*Butterfly, The Lonely Lady*

"There's nought, no doubt,
so much the spirit calms
As rum and true religion."

—George Noel Gordon,
Lord Byron,
"Don Juan"

Dear Paul,

in haste after a month's absence and a pile of mail..now on returning—all I can say is <u>where</u> is the evidence? All I see are dubiously evolved human beings dead-scared of their mortality (see Ernst Becker's book on the FEAR OF DEATH-I forget the exact title but the innumerable results-and his logic-are just about unarguable)...fabricating 1000's of different religions and 'gods" (based on fear) and it has not as yet impressed me- But who knows how desperate I may become...One thing I believe is how little we know about the physics and mathematics of the universe and therefore about life- and time and infinity and space and matter etc. Warmest regards and thanks for your intriguing note, idea, survey. Do let me know what Glen Campbell, Pat Boone, Pat Robertson (Club 700), Dale Evans, etc. say.

Salaams,

Peter
(Beard)

Peter (Beard)

PETER BEARD
Photographer, author, filmmaker   Author—*The End Game*, Film—*Longing for Darkness*

COSMOPOLITAN

Helen Gurley Brown, Editor · 224 West 57th Street, New York, New York, 10019, (212) 262-7916

February 14, 1977

Dear Paul,

It's hard to describe the kind of God I believe in because God, to me, is not a person or entity who sits out there making judgements. God is a kind of force that makes itself known by rewarding you for good work. "Good work" includes everything from working very industriously at your job to being a good friend to your friends, taking care of your family, being a good lover to the person you love ... when you pour everything into these endeavors, God—or this special force that is God—rewards you with very rich blessings ... more success in your job, more or deeper friendships, a happier family, a happier lover or whatever ... My particular god does not do bad things to anybody ... that's another force entirely. We have to come up with another definition of whatever that force is.

Sincerely,

Helen Brown

Master Paul Rifkin
333 W. Frances Willard
Chico, California 95926

HGB/pmq

HELEN GURLEY BROWN
Editor-in-chief, *Cosmopolitan* magazine, Author—*Sex and the Single Girl*

Yes

*through
faith,
& variation
See Bible*

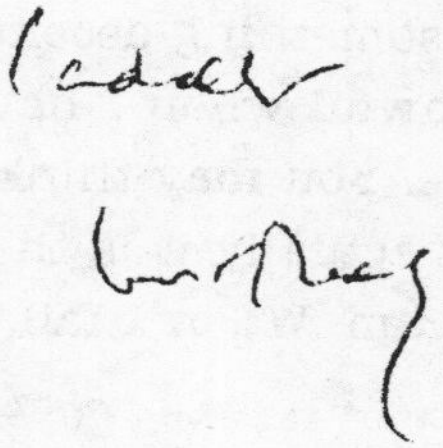

[handwritten signature]

WILLIAM F. BUCKLEY
Author, magazine editor
Author—*God and Man at Yale*, Host—*Firing Line*, Editor—*National Review*

San Francisco Chronicle

November 19, 1976

Dear Paul:

Thanks for your letter, and sorry to be so late replying.

Yes, I belive in God, for He makes me feel good when I have done something decent and generous, and He makes me feel awful when I have been mean, selfish, petty and vindictive. You may think I am talking about my conscience, but actually it is the spirit of God. I am trying to emulate Him. When I fail, He and I are disapppointed.

All best,

[signature]

HERB CAEN
Columnist, *San Francisco Chronicle*, Author—*Baghdad-by-the-Sea*

24 Sep 80

Dear Paul Rifkin =
 I believe in
goodness. I let others
believe in a god.

Sincerely,

Erskine Caldwell

ERSKINE CALDWELL
Author—*Tobacco Road, God's Little Acre*

The New York Times

229 WEST 43 STREET
NEW YORK, N.Y. 10036

March 3, 1983

Paul Rifkin
674 Route 6A
East Sandwich, Massachusetts 02537

Dear Paul:

Please forgive my long delay in answering your letter but I have been away from my desk and home for a prolonged period.

To answer your question, perhaps because I need to compensate for my feelings of failure and other shortcomings, I believe that there is are and always have been mystic forces acting in my behalf. Supernal beings. Among other things, as I have stated, I do believe in God, although I do not belong to any organized religion. I envision God as some vague, bearded, robed, paternal figure out of a Michelangelo painting, something perhaps from the frescoes in the Sistine Chapel. And when I am in need (even for trivial, small, material things) I pray to Him quietly and, perhaps because of my belief, which makes me act positively when I might have otherwise acted negatively, I often find my prayers answered.

I hope this answers your question.

Sincerely,

Craig Claiborne

CRAIG CLAIBORNE
Editor, author of cookbooks—*The New York Times Cookbook*

I do <u>not</u> believe in God, but I
am very interested in Him (Her?)!

Sincerely

Arthur C. Clarke

JUNE 1976.

ARTHUR C. CLARKE
Author—*The Nine Billion Names of God, 2001: A Space Odyssey*

UNIVERSITY OF CALIFORNIA, LOS ANGELES   UCLA

BERKELEY · DAVIS · IRVINE · LOS ANGELES · RIVERSIDE · SAN DIEGO · SAN FRANCISCO   SANTA BARBARA · SANTA CRUZ

DEPARTMENT OF PSYCHIATRY AND
BIOBEHAVIORAL SCIENCES

August 24, 1983

Paul Rifkin
674 Route 6A
East Sandwich, Mass. 02537

Dear Paul,

The fact that I am alive on the planet Earth in a Solar
System which is part of a galaxy in a universe in which
there are at least four trillion other galaxies is as much
evidence as I need or can absorb.

                              Sincerely,

                              Norman Cousins

NC/cpb

NORMAN COUSINS
Editor, *Saturday Review*
Author—*In God We Trust: The Religious Beliefs of the Founding Fathers*

JAMES DICKEY

September 22, 1980

Mr. Paul Rifkin
RFD #2—off Grant Road
Newmarket, New Hampshire 03857

Dear Paul,

Thank you very much for your letter.

In answer to your question — do I believe in God — I would say this: whatever made what is, from the sand grain to the galaxy, is worthy of <u>my</u> worship. Whether such a force as we call God knows anything about me or not, I don't know. I would say to God what the angels say to Him in Goethe's <u>Faust</u>:

> Thine aspect cheers the hosts of heaven
> Though what Thine essence, none can say.

Sincerely,

James Dickey

James Dickey

JAMES DICKEY
Poet, novelist, filmmaker, critic—*Deliverance, God's Images*

Dec 11, 1976

Dear Mr. Pickle!

What a pickle! To tell you whether I think there is God or Not?!

God is a Pickle. That is to say, any god you project is a projection (Perception, view etc) of Pickle.

If Pickle wants to be god, Pickle will be god. He'll be god maybe 10,000,000 years in the highest God Realms. But then he'll get sick of being Pickle.

So then he'll decide a permanent Self is not necessary.

Whew! No Pickle, no god, no ego, no claustrophobia! (No pressure.)

Take it easy

Allen Ginsberg

P.S. Just opened your letter today   P.S. Can you understand this in the 5th grade.

I owned land adjacent to Allen Ginsberg's in California—Feeling he would know my name, I wrote to him as 'Paul Pickle'

ALLEN GINSBERG
Poet—"Howl"

DEAR PAUL: I'M FLATTERED BY YOUR
ASKING ME, BUT I HAVE NEVER SEEN ANY
EVIDENCE OF THE EXISTENCE OF A SUPERNATURAL
BEING. THEREFORE, I DO NOT BELIEVE IN GOD.
ALL BEST,

RALPH GINZBURG
Editor, publisher—*Eros, Avant-Garde, Moneysworth*

CHARACTER
QUALITY
ENTERPRISE
ACCURACY

HEARST NEWSPAPERS

AMERICAN PAPERS FOR THE AMERICAN PEOPLE

959 EIGHTH AVE.   NEW YORK, N.Y. 10019

November 5, 1976

Paul Rifkin
4212 25th Street
San Francisco, California 94114

Dear Paul:

I do indeed believe in God!

While he has never made his presence "known" to me—as you put it—that is through any audible message or dream or appearance, I believe in Him because of what I have read of the life of Jesus Christ and His utterances as quoted in the Scriptures.

I think it was Voltaire, the famous Frenchman of letters and philosopher, who is credited with observing that "If God did not exist, man would find it necessary to invent Him."

What Voltaire meant by this cryptic remark was that throughout recorded time man has needed something to worship—some Supreme Being to believe in. Some people worship the sun, others the moon, others gold images of animals, while others have deified people who actually lived.

I'll give you one more quote which you can think about and which may help explain the existence of God. It was a phrase I heard constantly (author unknown) during World War II, and it went like this: "There are no atheists

WILLIAM RANDOLPH HEARST, JR.
Editor, executive director of Hearst Corporation

in foxholes." This means, in case it's a little obscure to a young person, that when you were under intense shellfire you had to burrow into the ground like an animal to give your body as much protection as possible, that little ditch was known as a foxhole. And when you had to do that and you were scared to death, chances are you prayed to God for your life; thus you were not an atheist.

Hope I made some constructive contribution to your philosophy of life.

Sincerely,

W.R. Hearst, Jr.

John Hersey R. F. D.,
Box 1607, Vineyard Haven, Massachusetts 02568

October 8, 1980.

Dear Paul Rifkin:

You've put a very hard question. I was brought up
the son of missionaries, in China, and when I was small
I think I was stifled by too much formal religion; I have
been skeptical of sectarian religion ever since. I think I
am an agnostic, though I have a powerful sense of the
mystery of the universe. When did it start? The scientists
say there was a "big bang," but they can't say what
happened before the big bang! And I am constantly
astonished, and deeply moved, by the wonderful complexity
of the natural world—so many intricate forms of life, so
much that is both beautiful and awesome. I don't believe
in an intelligence behind all this; it seems to me just to
have <u>happened</u> in some unaccountable way. Whatever the
way, I am very glad to be a small part of it all, to be alive!

Sincerely,

John Hersey

JOHN HERSEY
Author—*Hiroshima*

WILLIAM BRADFORD HUIE

P. O. Box 248
HARTSELLE, ALABAMA
35640

May 21, 1983

Dear Paul Rifkin....

It was kind of you to ask me such an important question. My reply has been delayed by my being away.

Very early in my long life I was taught to <u>respect life's mysteries</u>. Meaning that I have never been impressed by <u>how</u> <u>much</u> human beings know and can ever know about the miracles of life and the universe. I have instead been impressed by how little we can ever know and therefore how much we must rely on what we call <u>faith</u>.

So I am a man of <u>faith</u>, and my faith tells me that the miracles of life and the universe didn't <u>just</u> <u>happen</u>. There had to be a Creator.... a Creator whose appearance, size, shape, and place of abode man can never hope to understand or even imagine. This Creator men have called God, and I don't know any better name. So, yes, I believe in God.

Many human beings search for God in groups, others of us search alone. I have always been a <u>loner</u>. God has never made Himself known to me in any spectacular manner. But I have <u>felt</u> His presence many times. I suppose I have tried to <u>serve</u> God by showing respect for His creatures, His handiwork, and His mysteries.

May God bless you throughout your life.

Wm. B. Huie

WILLIAM BRADFORD HUIE
Author—*The Execution of Private Slovik, The Hiroshima Pilot*

20 April 1983

Dear Paul Rifkin:

In answer to your question, "Do you believe in God?" I can
only tell you this: during my life, I have met several dozen
people who, I am certain, really did believe in God. This
belief guided them throughout their lives and gave them
strength and made them happy. In fact, their happiness
was something wonderful and it seemed more powerful
than any misfortunes which they met with. So I can say,
at least, that I believe in their belief in God.

Sincerely,

Christopher Isherwood

Christopher Isherwood

April 1, 1983

Paul Rifkin
Grade 5
674 Route 6A
East Sandwich, Massachusetts 02537

Dear Paul Rifkin,

I received your letter regarding your fifth grade class survey on the existence of God.

Yes, I believe in God and He makes his presence known to me everytime I see the face of someone I love.

Sincerely,

Kitty Kelley

dec. 21, 1980

Dear Mr. Rifkin

I'm sorry to be so long answering your inquiry, and I'm sure I'm too late for your report. I have had to spend too much time running in and out of town this fall.

But, to answer your question briefly, yes, I do believe in God, mainly because of certain very strong personal intuitions of His presence. Together with an equally strong experience of answered prayer.

I could not deny these, or what I believe to be their source, and still be honest.

May I wish you all the luck for the holidays—and in your work?

Sincerely

Walter Kerr

WALTER KERR
Drama critic, Author—*God on the Gymnasium Floor*

Fletcher Knebel

208 Edgerstoune Road   Princeton, New Jersey 08540

Phone: (609) 924-2949

May 26, 1983

Dear Paul:

An eternal question, that one.

Whether or not I believe in God makes little difference in the grand scheme of things since my belief won't influence reality one iota. God either exists or it, he or she doesn't and nothing I think can change the fact.

Yet men have fought, killed and slaughtered one another on the premise that piles of human bodies would somehow prove their dubious theology.

My core belief on these eschatological matters is that no one knows. It is all a great mystery, unpierced by any man or woman since the dawn of human intelligence. Therefore when I hear some money-raising, shouting and ranting preacher proclaim this, that or the other theological certainty, I put him down as a scoundrel, an ignoramus or an honest man sadly misled by his own ego.

Here we are tiny specks on a pea-size planet, floating out in the boondocks of space in one of the billions of galaxies that make up this fantastically huge universe. For us to pretend that we know anything about the existence or non-existence of a superpower, why, it's ridiculous.

A friend, Monsignor Illich, a rebel mind in the Catholic church, was once asked why he continued in the church if he felt so alienated from its theology.

"To celebrate the mystery," he replied.

I too am often overcome with awe at the immensity of the unknowns and the vastness of this never-ending universe. It is all too much for our little minds to comprehend. So I have streaks of spirituality when I celebrate the mystery.

Do I believe in God? No. But what difference does that make? Would my belief prove anything?

Good luck, Paul. Keep asking the big questions.

All the best,

Fletcher Knebel

paul krassner
box 14667
san francisco 94114

Paul Rifkin
674 Route 6A
East Sandwich, Mass.

June 11

Dear Paul,

Thanks for your note. It is hard to say whether one believes in God because the concept is so vague. To me, God is a word that serves as a metaphor for the mystery of my relationship—every moment—with the universe. Thus, even if I am an atheist, I seem to have more of an ongoing intimacy with this deity that I don't believe in, than many who profess belief in God. Ultimately, it comes down to believing in yourself, since that is the only consciousness you have. Hope this is of some help to you. I would be interested in seeing a copy of your report.

Cordially

Paul Krassner

PAUL KRASSNER
Writer, editor—*The Realist*

*I believe in a sprituality
that binds each of us to
one another and relates
us by kinship with all
living things, the earth,
the sky and the universe.
I learned this from the American Indians I have represented.*

William H Kunstler

11/9/76

WILLIAM KUNSTLER
Lawyer, educator, ACLU director
Author—*And Justice for All*

GEORGE LEONARD

July 18, 1983

Dear Paul,

Your letter came while I was away for a two-month residency at Esalen Institute, so this reply is probably too late for your survey.

Nevertheless, I could say that I believe in the existence of a divine spirit. I'm not sure this spirit could be seen as a person, but is certainly at least personal. The divine spirit, which I might call "God," makes its presence known to me, not just at church or during religious services, but any time at all when I'm willing to open my heart to the wonders of existence; whenever, for example, I truly apprehend the essence of a tree or the flight of a swallow. Thus, God must exist in all of us as well as <u>apart from</u> us—both at once.

Let me wish you all good things in your life.

Sincerely,

George Leonard

GEORGE LEONARD
Author—*Education and Ecstasy*

141 rue de Rennes
Paris 75006
November 25, 1980

Dear Paul Ritkin:

I don't believe in God.

Sincerely,

Mary McCarthy

P.S. But I do believe in quite a lot of Christ's teaching.

April 15, 1983

Dear Paul-

Yes, I do believe in God. He has made his presence known to me through kind and loving people I have known—some of them happily close relatives of mine.

Sincerely yours,

Mary McGrory

April 7, 1983

Paul Rifkin
Grade 5
674 Rte. 6A
E. Sandwich, Mass. 02537

Dear Paul,

Thank you for your nice note. In reply to your question as to whether or not I believe in God . . . I think it would be very difficult to believe in one's self without acknowledging a supreme being or a higher order.

I feel God is manifested in the faces of the young and the very old. Proof of God is in the good things people do for each other. But it is not just in people—how can one pass a tree, see an animal or even look skyward without knowing that God is in the neighborhood somewhere.

Good luck on your report.

My best to you,

Rod McKuen

RM/cp

P.S. Enclosed is my book <u>An Out Stretched Hand</u> which explains my views of God even further.

Rod McKuen
P.O. Box G
Beverly Hills, CA 90213

ROD McKUEN
Poet, composer, author, singer
Poetry—*We Touch the Sky*, Film score—*The Prime of Miss Jean Brodie*

Dear Paul Rifkin,

Strange as it may seem, I believe God makes his/her presence known to me in everything, even in nothing. In the most terrible and in the most wonderful moments, that presence emanates. And if it's all in my head (or in a place imagined to be the soul which may be God imagining me) that Presence lights up my brain's dark ridges to reflect itself back onto the world. God (or what is named the energy connecting us to everything and even nothing) surrounds us from within and without.

I've always pondered the words "believe" and "know." Sometimes I find belief gets in the way of knowing.

I hope this has been helpful.

Sincerely,

David Meltzer.

DAVID MELTZER
Author, musician, poet
Editor—*Anthology of the Classic Kabbalah*

Steeple Aston   Oxford   June 5

Dear Paul,

Thank you for your letter. I don't believe in God, that
is I do not believe in a divine person or controlling intelligence.
But I believe in <u>religion</u> as spiritual change, response to a spiritual
reality. I think this is what Hindus and Buddhists believe. All
best wishes to you,

Iris Murdoch

IRIS MURDOCH
Author and philosopher, philosophy don at Oxford

KEMPIS

ORRISDALE ROAD

BALLASALLA.

ISLE OF MAN

CASTLETOWN 2440

Feast Day of
St John of
St Facundus
(12th June 1983)

Dear Paul Rifkin,

You write asking Do I believe in God? My dear chap, I think you must be a bit soft in the head to even ask a question like that. You might as well ask a whale does it believe in water, or a swallow in air. Who are we to believe or disbelieve? Anybody who only _believes_ in God must have something missing. If you don't feel our most dear and loving Creator in every breath you breathe, every step you take, every thought that crosses your mind, all I can say is, God help you.

We have each one of us a tiny speck of God within us, and our true purpose on earth is to keep that alive.

So stop asking daft questions.

Yours sincerely,

(I should not have replied had I known that this letter was for publication.)

BILL NAUGHTON
Author—_Alfie_

112

**SOCIAL
SCIENCE
INSTITUTE**

HARBORSIDE, MAINE

Dear Paul,

Answering your letter:

In any serious discussion of a question such as yours: "Do you believe in God?" it is customary for the one who propounds the question to state the question for discussion & define the terms.

Before I answer your question therefore, I would ask you to define terms & begin by answering my request by defining the term "God" as you are using it. As you know, the term has many & various meanings.

Very truly yours.

Scott Nearing,

—

SCOTT NEARING
Sociologist, Author—*Living the Good Life, The Conscience of a Radical*

Dear Mr. Nearing:

Thank you for responding to my survey. I define "God" as the energy that connects us all.

But I am much more interested in whether you believe in a God (of your own definition).

Thank you for participation in my project.
Sincerely,
P.R.

October 18, 1980

Dear Paul:

Thank you for your definition of God as "the energy that connects us all". That is an unusual and interesting definition.

I accept this definition, with a slight change. Omit "us", making it read: "the energy that connects all".

I suggest this because your definition as it stands seems to refer to human beings only. Taking out "us" makes it easier to include animals, flowers, rocks, trees and other aspects of nature that are part of the All.

Using that as my definition, yes, I believe in the universe as it is, in all its aspects. I also believe that the universe changes a bit each hour and each day, so there is an ever-changing All.

This makes possible an even shorter definition of our word God: "God Is". This wording makes God and Being mean essentially the same thing.

Hoping you will continue with your investigations,

Yours truly,

Scott Nearing,

SCOTT NEARING
Sociologist, Author—*Living the Good Life, The Conscience of a Radical*

LEN:	Do you believe in God?
MARK:	What?
LEN:	Do you believe in God?
MARK:	Who?
LEN:	God.
MARK:	God?
LEN:	Do you believe in God?
MARK:	Do I believe in God?
LEN:	Yes.
MARK:	Would you say that again?
LEN:	Have a biscuit.

From THE DWARFS by Harold Pinter

the village VOICE

New York's
Weekly Newspaper
842 Broadway
New York, N.Y.
10003
475-3300

November 21, 1980

Dear Paul,

Good luck on your project. I hope this answer isn't too late to be of help.

If indeed, as Carl Dreyer said, God is love—then I believe in God. And He has made His presence known to me very often in life though not in any way that could be called supernatural.

Sincerely,

Andrew Sarris

Andrew Sarris

ANDREW SARRIS
Film critic, *Village Voice*
Author—*The Primal Screen*

Yes
Many events in my life have no explanation
except God's hand.

PHYLLIS SCHLAFLY
Lawyer
Author—*The Power of the Positive Woman*

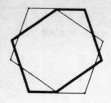

The Graduate School and University Center
of the City University of New York

Albert Schweitzer Chair in the Humanities
Graduate Center 33 West 42 Street, New York, N.Y. 10036
212 790-4261

April 12, 1977

Paul Rifkin
333 W. Frances Willard
Chico, California 95926

Dear Paul:

I believe that there is an ultimate mystery in the universe—a mystery that must constantly remind us all of the finitude of man, the limits of human wisdom and to call that mystery God, it is OK by me.

Sincerely yours,

Arthur Schlesinger, jr.

ARTHUR SCHLESINGER, JR.
Educator, special assistant to President Kennedy
Author—*A Thousand Days*

CABLE NEWS NETWORK
2133 Wisconsin Ave., N.W./Washington, D.C. 20007/202-298-7400

Daniel Schorr

MEMORANDUM

to _____ Paul Rifkin _____ date __ Oct. 18 __

I AM HAPPY ABOUT YOUR RESPECT, THOUGH I DO NOT
CONSIDER MYSELF A FAMOUS PERSON. THOUGH I WOULD
LIKE VERY MUCH TO ANSWER YOUR QUESTION, IT IS
HARD FOR ME TO DO SO. THERE ARE SOME THINGS THAT I
CONSIDER VERY PERSONAL—MY RELIGIOUS FEELINGS, IN
THE FIRST PLACE, AND EVEN HOW I VOTE. I HOPE IT WILL
NOT LESSEN YOUR RESPECT FOR ME.

Sincerely

Daniel Schorr

DANIEL SCHORR
Journalist
Author—*Clearing the Air* Emmy awards for coverage of Watergate scandal

HUBERT SELBY, JR.

139 NORTH LA JOLLA AVENUE

LOS ANGELES, CALIFORNIA 90048

TELEPHONE (213) 655-8582

November 24, 1976

Paul Rifkin
4212 - 25 Street
San Francisco, Calif. 94114

Dear Paul:

I just received your letter and thank you for the compliment. To be known and respected by a 5th grader is humbling and extremely flattering.

I assume from the fact that you are in the 5th grade that you are about 10 years old, but have no intention of talking to you as an adult to a child. You have asked the most important question in the world and are, therefore, a person that does not need to be talked, "down" to because of his age.

Yes, I do believe in God. I also believe that an individuals relationship with God is the most important thing in their life.

God made his presence known to me, I guess, in many ways, all of which can be summed up in the word, LOVE. He loved me enough to allow me to make all the mistakes I could make and never once chastised me or frowned upon me.

He allowed me to follow the path of self-will where I constantly ended up in the black pit of despair.

He allowed me to do all the things I knew in my heart and soul a man should not do, the very things I always said I would never do, yet he always helped me out of the pit of degradation and self-loathing, never once punishing me.

He allowed me to hate and despise Him for many long and painful years of my life, He allowed me to damn, defy and deny him and still no matter what I did all He ever did was love me.

He allowed me to find out in my own way that a man is not a guy who attains wordly success, but that a real Man, is a guy who can humble himself before God.

HUBERT SELBY, JR.
Author—*Last Exit to Brooklyn, The Room*

He allowed me to find out all these things in my own way and in my own time and then when I finally ran out of energy and stopped hating him for a moment He stepped in and turned the direction of my life around.

God allowed me to find out in my way and my time that happiness is a process of elimination, the ultimate elimination being a life based on self-centeredness. I tried every way I could to find happiness, and, as I said, He never stopped me. It was only by trying all my methods that I was able to eventually accept the fact that God is the only answer, the only reality, the only truth, that in His Will is our Peace, that it is indeed true that God is Love and that Love is the greatest thing in the world.

God continues to make His presence known to me in many ways, but some of the personal ways are a feeling of peace and contentment; a feeling of inner security and serenity of purpose; a feeling of hope; by intuitively giving me the answers to questions that absolutely baffled me in the past; by helping me try to have a reverence for all of His creation; by giving me a desire to seek Him; and by turning my hatred into a love affair ...a love affair with my God.

I hope this letter fulfills your needs and desires, to some extent at least. If you have any other questions I will be happy to try and answer them for you.

I hope you and your family have a happy Holiday Season, and enjoy the blessings of Gods love.

Love,

H. Selby. Jr.

Dear Paul Rifkin
My answer is: No.
God. for me, is the entire universe.

Friendly yours

[signature] 27 avril 1983.

GEORGES SIMENON
Belgian novelist—212 novels (80 in the Maigret detective series)

Stahl

Mr. Paul Rifkin
East Sandwich
Mass. U.S.A.

Dear Paul:
Thank you for the honor of being included in your list of famous people.
The answers that you will receive I am sure will be most interesting.
It is quite a question!

It seems to me that your fifth grade class must be remarkable. In my
fifth grade class a momentous question would be . . . Do you think
that the New York Yankees will win the pennant?

To your question, "Do you believe in God?" my answer is a qualified
yes. And it would be easier for me to tell you what I think
God is not rather than tell you what I think God is. For an example
. . . my God does not have a long, white beard and He doesn't live in
a place called Heaven. He knows all about me the same way he
knows all about the wind blowing a branch of a tree. Both, the wind
and I being a part of His Grand Plan. To me He has no physical
substance . . . He is idea. He is not likely to walk into your classroom,
his long robes flowing, and say, "Hi Paul!" Yet, using a set of iron-
clad laws, he runs the entire universe, from the tiniest speck of matter
to the largest sun. To a human there is always a start and a finish.
To Him, there is no beginning . . . no end. I often refer to Him as
"Nature", and he certainly gives me a lot to think about. For which
I am grateful.

Very truly yours,

Ben Stahl

Ben Stahl
April 22, 1983

BEN STAHL
Artist, author, Illustrator

No. I believe in the still undiscovered and perhaps infinite possibilities of human beings and nature that we sometimes personify as God.

GLORIA STEINEM
Writer, lecturer, feminist, cofounder and editor of *Ms* magazine

NBC News   A Division of
National Broadcasting Company, Inc.

May 12, 1983

Paul Rifkin
674 Route 6A
East Sandwich, Massachusetts 02537

Dear Paul:

Thank you for your recent letter. I am flattered that you thought to write to me.

Yes, I do believe that there is some force greater than the individual that leads human beings and some other living things to operate beyond <u>self</u>-interest. I guess that is what we call God.

God is revealed to me in the goodness of others.

Also, I think you are on the right track when you ask how God made his presence known to me. In framing the question that way, you recognize that religious beliefs come from a lifetime of personal experience, and that a person should not tell his neighbor what to believe.

It was nice to hear from you.

Sincerely,

Carl Stern
NBC News-Washington

CARL STERN
News correspondent, lawyer

✿ WFMT

CHICAGO'S FINE ARTS STATION / 98.7

March 4, 1977

Paul Rifkin
333 West Francis Willard
Chico, Calif. 95926

Dear Paul,

I believe there is a God in every person; you, me, all on this earth. His presence is known to me by the fact that we are alive and breathing and thinking.

Yours,

Studs Terkel

St/mt

STUDS TERKEL
Interviewer, Author—*Hard Times*

127

OCT. 28, 1975

Dear MR. Thompson:

I am making a survey of Famous people I respect for a 5th Grade Class Report

My question to you is:

DO YOU BELIEVE IN GOD?

[If the answer is Yes, please describe how God mAde His presence known to you].

Thank you in advance for your reply.

Sincerely
Paul RIFKIN
Grade 5
4212 25th St.
San Francisco
CALIF 94114

No — but I'm not always right, and

I don't think it matters much anyway.

HUNTER S. THOMPSON
Author—*Fear and Loathing in Las Vegas*

425 NORTH MICHIGAN AVENUE · CHICAGO, ILLINOIS 60611

November 12, 1980

Dear Paul:

Thank you for your nice letter.
I do believe in God.
But I cannot tell you how He has made His presence known to me. I do not think He has ever made His presence known to me. However, that is not necessary for me to believe in Him.
Perhaps the existence of the world itself is the best evidence for the existence of God. Someone must have made the world. Who could that have been other than God?
But as I say this is all unnecessary. I believe in God without having any evidence of his existence. I believe God exists because He must exist.

Yours sincerely,

Charles Van Doren

CHARLES VAN DOREN
Author—*The Idea of Progress,* Editor—*Encyclopaedia Britannica*

IRVING WALLACE

Oct. 21, 1980

Dear Paul,

No.

Irving Wallace

IRVING WALLACE
Author—*The Chapman Report, The Intimate Sex Lives of Famous People*

April 14, 1983

Dear Paul Rifkin,

God made his presence known to me through the words and acts of my parents . .

They were Quaker, as I am, and were accustomed to reading the Bible praying, and following the commandments of Jesus. Through their example the presence and existence of God was made known to me.

Thank you for your letter.

Best wishes,

Jessamyn West

JESSAMYN WEST
Author—*The Quaker Reader, The Friendly Persuasion*

The New York Times

229 WEST 43 STREET
NEW YORK, N.Y. 10036

TOM WICKER
ASSOCIATE EDITOR

December 31, 1976

Mr. Paul Rifkin
4212 25th Street
San Francisco, California

Dear Paul:

This is a long delayed reply to your letter of November 1 about my religious views.

I cannot give you a brief or specific answer because I do not have strongly formulated or long-formed religious attitudes. As a child, I was forced by my family into a typical religious pattern within the Methodist Church; since then, I have scarcely attended church at all, but I would not say I have no religion.

I'm sorry if this seem inadequate, but I have to say that my primary concern has been ethical behavior in life rather than religious faith. Mysticism has no appeal to me, nor the idea of an afterlife.

Sincerely,

Tom Wicker

TOM WICKER
Journalist, associate editor—*The New York Times*, Author—*Tears Are for Angels*

Boston University

College of Liberal Arts
232 Bay State Road, Boston, Massachusetts 02215

Department of Political Science

November 5, 1980

Dear Paul:

Do I believe in God? If that means: do I believe in one Supreme Being who bears responsibility for everything that happens, and to whom we should pray for the things we need, and whose will is presented to us by priests, ministers, rabbis, and various churches and synagogues and sacred documents—then my answer is no.

If believing in God means believing there is mystery in the universe, there is much that is unknown, there is a spiritual quality to things which cannot be expressed in words, that love among human beings is the most important thing in the world, that all men are brothers and all women are sisters and all human beings should respect one another, and that it is up to us to act (not to pray) to bring about a state of love and brotherhood and sisterhood—well, then, you would have to say I believe in that .

I'm sorry to give you such a complicated answer to a simple question, but that's the only way I can answer it! Best of luck in your survey.

Howard Zinn
Howard Zinn

HOWARD ZINN
Historian, educator, Author—*Disobedience and Democracy*

Athletes

"The gods play games with men as balls."

—Plautus
"Captivi"

Dear Paul:

      Yes I do believe in God. I have always been a fairly faithful Catholic but in 1979 I had an experience which has brought me even closer.

      I made a Cursillio in Oct. 1979, and at this retreat I experienced the presence of our Lord. I looked back over my life and realized that it was Him who gave me the gift to play football and it was Him who had it end for me because of an injury. I feel it was for the purpose of moving on and doing more of His work with the people who I have an influence on and that is what has happen since the Cursillio.

                    With friendship,

                    Dick Butkus

P.S. You have good penmanship for a 5th grader.

DICK BUTKUS
Middle linebacker, Chicago Bears—named to Pro Football Hall of Fame

Paul

Yes I believe in god
Just Look UP
in the Sky
Do you think that
Man could have put
that together
?

Best Wishes

Roy Campanella

ROY CAMPANELLA
Catcher, Brooklyn Dodgers (1949–58)—named to Baseball Hall of Fame
Author—*It's Good to Be Alive*

UNIVERSITY OF NOTRE DAME

Football Office

GERRY FAUST
Head Football Coach

J.M.J.
June 8, 1983

Paul Rifkin
674 Route 6A
East Sandwich, Massachusetts 02537

Dear Paul:

In answer to your question, "Do you believe in God?" Yes, I do. God is present everywhere you look—in the people you deal with, in the beautiful trees and flowers and plants, in the whole universe.

I don't feel that I could live without God. Even though I've hit some tough times, He has always helped me out of adversity. I always thank God for what He has given me and don't dwell on what I don't have. I really feel that if you're thankful for what you have and never worry about what you don't have, you'll always be a happy person in life. God has been exceptionally good to me in my life, and every day I try to thank Him for what He has done for me.

I hope that all goes well for you. May God bless you always.

Yours in Notre Dame,

GERRY FAUST

ks

GERRY FAUST
Head football coach, Notre Dame

Dear Sir;

I got your letter. And the answer to your question is, yes. In March 1977, after my last boxing match on returning to the dressing room I lost my life yes, DIED, I in a moment time, I was in a deep dark empty place, For years there had been talks about God but without real belief, But without hope in, such a sad dark place, I said, I do not care if this is death I still believe in God. When I spoke dose words there was once again life in my body. So happy to be alive screamed I Am dying for God.

Then with out control I started reciting the Bible how Jesus had died on the cross and was stell alive today. I even saw on my head, feet and hands the blood where he was wounded.

I retired from boxing. To day I preach.

Truely yours

George Foreman

Marty Liquori

Dear Paul,

    What famous people believe about God should not influence your belief. I will say that I don't think God will make his presence known to you in any visible way, and probably never has to anyone.

Regards,

Marty Liquori

MARTIN LIQUORI
Athlete, business executive, elite miler
Sportscaster—ABC, President of Athletic Attic, Inc.

Stirling Moss Limited

SM/SP   28th April, 1983.

Master Paul Rifkin,
Grade 5,
674 RT 6A.,
East Sandwich,
Mass 02537,
U.S.A.

Dear Paul,

Thanks very much for your letter asking about my belief in God.

Yes, I do believe in God but I cannot explain all the reasons in a few moments or on paper.

Life is complex and the world around us, its' beginning, continuance and end are all beyond my understanding, but I do feel that the Maker has to exist.

Yours sincerely,

Stirling Moss

Stirling Moss

ARNOLD PALMER ENTERPRISES

- POST OFFICE BOX FIFTY-TWO
- YOUNGSTOWN, PENNA. 15696
- AREA CODE 412 537-7751

ARNOLD PALMER
PRESIDENT

January 10, 1977

Paul Rifkin
4212 25th Street
San Francisco, California 94114

Dear Paul:

Sorry for taking so long to write back to you. I have been in Florida for the past three months and just had an opportunity to see your letter.

In response to your question, it seems like I have always felt God's presence in my life.

I hope this is satisfactory and that your survey is successful.

Best wishes to you and your family.

Sincerely,

Arnold Palmer

AP:kld

ARNOLD PALMER
Professional golfer

Floyd Patterson

P. O. BOX 336
NEW PALTZ, N. Y. 12561

Mr. Paul Rifkin   July 23, 1983
Grade 5
674 Route 6A
East Sandwich, MA 02537

Dear Paul:

I am writing in response to your recent letter about "How God Made His Presence Known To You.", and you can use the following:

First, let me say that I consider myself very lucky and at the same time very different from most people. That is, I was able to choose my religion and as a teenager I was baptised. The experience of not simply practicing a religion I was born into makes me appreciate being a Catholic all that much more. No matter what religion one believes in . . . it is especially rewarding when one truly loves what they choose to believe.

As regards how God made his presence known to me I must say that I developed an "awareness" at the same time that I chose my religion. The time came when I started to realize what death actually meant. As a child, it looked like something in a cowboy movie or a deep sleep. But as I grew older I became aware that it is much different. I could not and will not believe that we simply begin and end. Love is a unique phenomena. It makes those that feel it and those that give it realize that laws and rules do not define good and bad, right or wrong. The feelings of love make one "aware" of the feelings of good and bad. That phenomena has always touched me and guided me and convinces me that it's much too powerful, enduring and complicated to grow from flesh and bones . . . which do and will die. Everytime I think about death and everytime I feel love . . . I thank God.

Sincerely,

Floyd Patterson

Floyd Patterson

FLOYD PATTERSON
Boxer—former heavyweight champion of the world

June 2, 1983

Mr. Paul Rifkin
674 Route 6-A
East Sandwich, Massachusetts 02537

Dear Paul:

I certainly believe in God as who else would make the world as it is.

Best wishes and have a good summer.

Sincerely,

Digger Phelps (signature)

"Digger" Phelps
Head Basketball Coach

**BILL RODGERS
RUNNING CENTER**

April 27, 1983

Dear Paul,

    I believe in God in a personal way—not so much the way he's described by certain religions—

          See you on the roads one day—

Bill Rodgers

May 7, 1983

Mr. Paul Rifkin
674 Route 6A
East Sandwich, Massachusetts 02537

Dear Paul,

Thank you for your note and interest in responding to a survey you're
conducting in your fifth grade class. I hope that this letter will give you
all of the answers you had requested.

Do I believe in God? I most certainly do! It wasn't until I became a born
again Christian in 1972 that I really believed in God and met His Son
Jesus Christ. In essence, that is what happens when you become a born again
Christian. I have enclosed a little magazine with a story related to this
that will probably help you understand more about what I am saying.

God has indeed blessed me with a wonderful talent to run. He has also given
me a marvelous wife and four happy healthy children. I have Him to be
thankful for. Have you ever met God? Have you ever asked Jesus Christ to
come into your life and to make you a born again Christian? It's very simple
and the end of this letter will explain just how you can do that. In the Bible
read John 3:3-8.

Now to your second question. How had God made His presence known to
me by circumstances and events. Once you put God first place in your
life then all other things fall in place. For example. As a runner I thought
that my identity as an individual was based upon my success in racing
the one mile distance. With that sort of thinking I always felt I had to continue
to excel or my identity would be taken away if someone achieved the
same thing I did. When I would achieve in a race that which I felt I was
capable of I would have peace in my life. That peace can best be described

JIM RYUN
Runner—former record holder for the mile

as a calmness and a moment of relaxation in knowing that everything was O.K. However that peace would disappear once I realized again that I must keep pressing on and excelling in my sport or my identity might be taken away. In May of 1972 when I became a born again Christian I received that kind of peace permanently. I no longer have to excel in sports and think that to be my identity. God knows my name and in fact in my mother's womb knew that I would someday be a runner. I know God exists for many other reasons, another one I would like to share with you.

The second example relates to the fact that I very much enjoy being involved in sports and athletics in particular running. I expressed to the Lord a number of years ago that desire and He has returned to me an opportunity to run again (I had retired for a period of time.) as well as encourage others to take care of their bodies physically. He has done this because I have been willing to serve Him in speaking to others throughout the world and sharing with them about Jesus Christ. God generally works through circumstances although he is at His best in working miracles in individual's lives. I know from personal experience and from others who have shared their experiences that they have seen God miraculously heal them and heal them of physical problems or financial problems.

I hope this letter has been of help to you. God be with you.

Sincerely,

Jim Ryun
John 3:3-8

"They that wait upon the Lord shall renew their strength... they shall run and not be weary..." Isaiah 40:31

NOV 9 1976

Nov 9 1976

Dear Paul:

I am very happy that you wrote to me, and that I am on your list of favorite people. I certainly do believe in God, and I'm only sorry that you are growing up at a time when some people say they have lost sight of Him. Maybe they aren't looking hard enough! I'm glad that you are, and I also hope that you and the rest of your fifth grade will continue to care very much about America and her leaders.

Your letter was one of the more important happenings in my day, and I want to thank you again for writing.

With warm regards,

Sincerely,

William E. Simon

Mr. Paul Rifkin
4212 25th Street
San Francisco, CA 94114

Enclosure

WILLIAM E. SIMON
Chairman of the U.S. Olympic Comm., Secretary of the Treasury, 1974–77

HOLLOWAY-STAUBACH CO., REALTORS ®

INVESTMENT REAL ESTATE

Roger T. Staubach
PRESIDENT

November 11, 1980

Paul Rifkin
Grade 5
674 Route 6-A
East Sandwich, Mass. 02537

Dear Paul:

I appreciated your letter regarding your class report.

Yes, I do believe in God.

My parents gave me a good Christian background in our home by teaching me and also through example and, I attended Catholic schools and church, which I still do.

I can't remember when I didn't have a belief in God and Jesus Christ, but it has become stronger and more real to me over the years. It has only been through my faith in God that I have been able to get through some very tough times in my life.

Thank you for writing.

Sincerely,

Roger Staubach

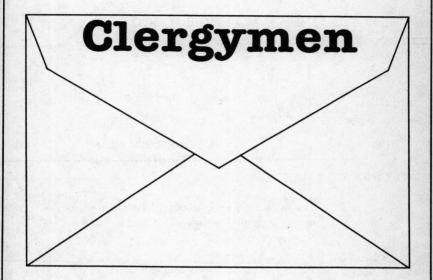

Clergymen

"THERE IS NO GOD BUT GOD."

—The Koran

"He that loveth not, knoweth not God:
God is love."

—The Holy Bible
First Epistle of John

"Men never do evil so completely and
cheerfully as when they do it from
religious conviction."

—Blaise Pascal
Lettres Provinciales

June 3, 1983

Dear Paul,

Sri Chinmoy is away on a trip, but when we told him about your fifth grade class report, he asked us to write you without delay so you wouldn't have to wait.

Yes, Sri Chinmoy believes in God. He not only believes in God but also sees God and talks to God all the time. In fact, God is now his very best friend.

Sri Chinmoy got to know God because he prays and meditates. He and God first became friends, very close friends, when Sri Chinmoy was 12 years old, just a few years older than you. That's when God first spoke to him during meditation. Since then, God has come to visit Sri Chinmoy many, many times and they have lots of conversations.

God can also become your best friend, Paul, if you also pray and meditate. Prayer is very simple. When you meditate, you become very quiet and just listen while God talks to you. When you pray and meditate, you see how much God loves you. He loves you even more than your parents love you, and you know how much they love you.

God wants you to become His dearest friend. So if you pray and meditate every day, you and God can become wonderful friends and talk together all the time. You can ask your parents to show you how.

Sincerely,

Chidananda

Chidananda

SRI CHINMOY
Religious leader

153

June 3, 1983

Paul Rifkin
674 Route 6A
East Sandwich, MA. 02537

Dear Paul:

It's late at night, and I'm trying to catch up on the mail. It may also be too late for this letter to help you with your fifth grade class report.

Yes, I do believe in God, and God has made his (or Her) presence known to me in Bach's b minor Mass, in Verdi's Requiem, and Dostoievsky's <u>Crime and Punishment</u>, in the face of my father and uncle and friends, but most of all, in the face of Jesus whom I see as the window through whom we see as much as is given to our mortal eyes to see of God. I don't think God is confined to Christ, but to me as a Christian, God is most essentially defined by Christ.

For many years I visited my aunt further to the Cape in Yarmouthport. I know exactly where East Sandwich is, and I hope you'll soon be out on those great dunes.

Very sincerely to you, too, Paul,

Bill

William Sloan Coffin

WILLIAM SLOANE COFFIN
Minister—Riverside Church, New York, N.Y.

154

May 10, 1983

Paul Rifkin
Grade 5
674 Route 6A
East Sandwich
MA 02537

Dear Paul:

Yes, I do believe in God, whose presence God has made known to me in the love people have shown me, and still do; in the Bible; and in the vastness and intricacy of nature.

All the best,

Harvey Cox (RT)

Harvey G. Cox

rt

HARVEY G. COX
Theologian—Professor of Divinity at Harvard
Author—*God's Revolution and Man's Responsibility*

Billy James Hargis Ministries, P.O. Box 977, Tulsa, Ok 74102

March 30, 1983

Paul Rifkin
Grade 5
674 Route 6A
East Sandwich, MA 02532

Dear Paul:

Please forgive me for not having answered your welcomed letter earlier than this. I have been very busy and have gotten behind, therefore, I am slow in answering you.

You asked me the question, "Do you believe in God?" I most certainly do. I believe in a personal God. I was an orphan. I never knew my real parents. A wonderful Christian couple in Texas by the name of Jimmy and Lucille Hargis, gave me a home and gave me a name. When I was 21 years of age, I legally became their adoptive son. They were so good to me—no real mother or father could have been nicer than my mother and dad. They went to church every Sunday. Although they didn't have the benefit of a formal education, they were experienced in life and were very smart people. My dad was a truck driver and a farmer and my mother was a housewife. They read the Bible every night before retiring. We prayed before every meal and went to church on Sunday morning and Sunday night.

I was ordained to the ministry when I was 17 years old. I have been in the ministry 40 years.

BILLY JAMES HARGIS
Clergyman
Author—*Why I Fight for a Christian America* and *Riches and Prosperity through Christ*

156

When I was a youngster attending elementary school I was aware of the presence of God. I remember how I would hum and sing the words of "Jesus is all the World to Me" during exam time. I felt that if I could be a minister it would be the greatest thing that I could do—the highest calling that a man could ever have. I wanted to be a minister so much and I was so thankful that my church felt that I was ready for it at age 17.

God has made His presence known to me by supernatural acts. I mean that too. I know that God answers prayer because there is seldom a week in my life that some prayer hasn't been answered. It couldn't be just an amazing happening. I know that God has answered my prayers. Because of my crusade against Communism and frequent trips that I have made to troubled spots of the world even behind the Iron Curtain—I have had several close calls but I was always supernaturally cared for by God. I believe in God because of supernatural events that I have experienced and could have only been the result of answered prayer.

God has revealed Himself to me through answered prayer. He has revealed Himself to me through the love of a mother and dad and the love of a wonderful wife and four children. He revealed Himself to me by giving me the idea for a unique ministry—"for Christ and against Communism" ministry when I started Christian Crusade.

There is an overriding belief in my life that Christ is coming back. I have never doubted the existence of God. Even when I did wrong and was punished for it and when things went wrong for me, I accepted it as the will of God., according to Romans 8:28.

God bless you, Paul, and best wishes.

I am

Yours in Christ,

Billy James Hargis

SUFI ORDER

Pir Vilayat Inayat Khan
Head of the Sufi Order

1570 PACHECO
SANTA FE, N.M. 87501
(505) 988-4411

June 13, 1983

Paul Rifkin
674 Route 6A
East Sandwich, MA 02537

Dear Paul,

I like challenging questions. Out of my scruple to avoid brainwashing my pupils, I always prefer encouraging people to get into a state where they can experience the divine qualities trying to come through their being, and the divine glance through their eyes, rather than locking them into a belief system.

Yours in His service,

Pir Vilayat Inayat Khan

PVIK:k

PIR VILAYAT INAYAT KHAN
Head of the Sufi order

FOUNDATION FOR CHRISTIAN LIVING

PAWLING, NEW YORK 12564

NORMAN VINCENT PEALE
Editor

December 27, 1976

Paul Rifkin
4212 25th St.
San Francisco, CA 94114

Dear Paul,
  Thank you for your letter.
  In answer to your question, God made His presence known to me when I made the decision to love Him, follow Him and do His will.
  He has become nearer with every passing day.

Cordially yours,

Norman Vincent Peale

NVP:ao

NORMAN VINCENT PEALE
Clergyman, Author—*The Power of Positive Thinking* and *Sin, Sex and Self-Control*

Ma Anand Sheela
D.Litt. (RIMU), Acharya

Personal Secretary to Bhagwan Shree Rajneesh

June 3, 1983
902.pn

Paul Rifkin
Grade 5
674 Route 6A
East Sandwich, MA 02537

Beloved Paul,

Love.

Thank you for your recent letter to Bhagwan.

"The fish is not thirsty in the sea, but man is. God is the
sea—God surrounds you, within and without. All that is,
is divine. God is not a person: God is the presence that is
overflowing everywhere in all directions. The radiance, the
beauty of existence, the splendor, and majestic, the
miraculous, the mysterious—the whole magic of life is God."*

His blessings,

Ma Anand Sheela

* from THE FISH IN THE SEA IS NOT THIRSTY
1980, Rajneesh Foundation International

BHAGWAN SHREE RAJNEESH
Religious leader

November 16, 1976
fs

Mr. Paul Rifkin
4212 25 St
San Francisco, CA 94114

Dear Paul:

Let me begin my letter by telling you this—the greatest gift God every gave man is Himself. He came to us in the form of His own Son. And it's an exciting fact for you and every need you face.

I once had a vision in which my sons were involved. In the vision one of them was picked up by rough men and carried away. I rushed after them but wasn't able to find them until later in the evening. And they had nailed my son to a cross. I rushed up and pulled him down, and he died in my arms with my name on his lips. In the vision God said, "How many sons have you, Oral Roberts?" I said, "Two." He said, "I only had one and I gave Him." I began to understand and said, "There isn't a human being that is worth the life of Your Son." He said, "You have no right to decide that. I say every human being is worth the death of My Son. That's what every person is worth." That was in 1951 and it marked my thinking about the value of people. I came into realization that every human being is worth something beyond my own ability to calculate, because who can estimate the worth of God's only begotten Son? He was God's seed planted to bring the miracle He wanted. We're all important to God. He loves us all. And nothing can take that love away from you or from me (Romans 8:38-39).

My darling wife, Evelyn, and I are very interested in you. We're interested in you because you took time to write us. We have a ministry of prayer. When we receive a letter from you, we pray, and we write you back. It's a ministry we have with people all over the world. And I lovingly give you an invitation to write me often. Write what's in your heart. I'll write you back every time. And I believe God will give you a new hold on life.

Now, may God abundantly bless you. And I believe He will.

Your prayer partner,

Oral Roberts

ORAL ROBERTS
Minister, founder of Oral Roberts University

Satchidananda Ashram - Yogaville, Inc.
A Tax Exempt, Non-Profit, Non-Sectarian Religious Organization

Sri Gurudev:
Rev. Swami Satchidananda

Route 1, Box 172
Buckingham, Virginia 23921
(804) 969-4801

Paul Rifkin
674 Route 6A
East Sandwich, Mass. 02537

8 July 1983

Dear Paul,

Hari Om! Swamiji sends you his love and blessings. He was very happy to receive your letter and to hear of the interesting project you are working on in summer school.

Swamiji does believe in God. In his biography, he gives a description of his experience of God's presence. This is what he says:

"My highest experience, which was not connected with any particular form, was the experience of Adwaita or Oneness or Enlightenment. I had that in 1949, a few months after my sannyas (monkhood) initiation. It was in mid-winter, when I visited Vasishta Cave. Vasishta was a great rishi, a sage who lived hundreds of years ago. There is a legend that it was in this cave he performed his austerities.

"I went into the cave, bending down until, after 25 feet, I reached a large room-like place with a seat. As I sat there and meditated, I had the experience of transcending my body and mind, realizing myself as the Omnipresent. I forgot my individuality. It is impossible to explain exactly what this is.

"I must have spent several hours in that state. Then I heard a humming sound, OM chanting, coming from a long distance away. Slowly, slowly, it became louder. As it neared, I became aware of my mind and body. I stood up and went out of the cave.

"For some time, I couldn't see anything in the normal way. All over I saw light, light, light. The whole world appeared to be a mass of light. There was only peace and peace everywhere. The state persisted that whole day.

SATCHIDANANDA
Religious leader, yogi

"Of course, after that, I had this experience very often, mostly when I visited a holy place. I had it in Badrinath and almost every day when I went to Mt. Kailash. I had it in Amarnath in Kashmir. Even in Ceylon, whenever I visited Adam's Peak. I had it in Jerusalem and at St. Peter's in the Vatican."

Swamiji speaks of God as the Peace within, a pure and steady peace that nothing can ever disturb. He also speaks of God as the raidant Light that illumines the entire universe and resides in the hearts of all.

At the Ashram (yoga center) where he lives, we are presently building a shrine dedicated to that Light. It is called LOTUS which stands for Light of Truth Universal Shrine. It will be situated alongside a lake and be in the shape of a beautiful lotus flower. Inside each of its twelve petals there will be an altar to one of the world's major religions and two of the petals will be for all other known and unknown religions. In the center of the temple will be a light that will radiate upwards and then split into twelve rays and shine down to illuminate the twelve altars. This will clearly illustrate the principle that all religions come from the one God. We sometimes like to say, "Truth is One, Paths are Many." The projected completion date for the shrine is July 1984.

If you or your friends are ever travelling in this area, please give us a call and come visit. We have a beautiful school that eighteen children now attend. We are situated on 700 acres and about 60 people now live here. There are various activities always going on, such as yoga programs, small businesses, gardening, and construction. It's a very interesting place to live. You learn how to live harmoniously with many people from different backgrounds and how to live in harmony with Nature, too.

We wish you all success on your school project and all peace and joy always.

Yours in Yoga,

Swam Karunananda Ma

Swami Karunananda Ma

Missionaries of Charity
                    54-A, Lower Circular Road
                    Calcutta - 700 016

                    8 / 5 / '83

Mr. Paul Rifkin
Grade 5
674 Route 6 A
East Sandwich, Mass. 02537

Dear Paul,

Thank you for your letter.

Yes, I believe in God and in His presence with us
in the world to-day. Faith is more important to me
than life itself because without it there would be no
fullness of life. I would be disposed to give my life
rather than my faith.

Our life and work as Missionaries of Charity are
built on faith - faith in Christ who said "I was
hungry, I was naked, I was sick and I was homeless,
and you took care of me" God has made His
presence known to us in the poor. He comes to us
as the hungry one, the sick one, the unwanted one
and gives us the chance to love Him and serve Him
in the distressing disguise; it is the same Christ
who is in all of us. Let us recognise Him and love
Him in one another even as He loved us-until it
hurt. Assuring you of our prayers and those of our
poor.

God bless you
Mc Teresa

MOTHER TERESA
Nobel Peace Prize Winner
Founder of the Missionaries of Charity

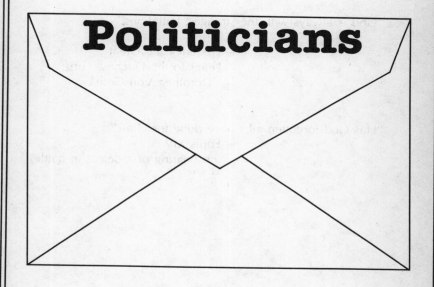

Politicians

"God is always with the strongest battalions"

—Frederick the Great
Letter to the Duchess Luise
Dorothea Von Gotha

"Has God forgotten all I have done for Him?"
—Louis XIV
(on hearing of a defeat in battle)

The State Senate
Atlanta

Julian Bond
SENATOR
THIRTY-NINTH DISTRICT

February 7, 1977

Dear Mr. Rifkin:

Thanks for your letter. I do believe in a higher order.

God has never made "His presence known to me" in any formal sense; I've had no visions or mystical experiences. I simply believe.

Sincerely,

Julian Bond

Julian Bond

JB/bc
enc.

Mr. Paul Rifkin
333 W. Frances Willard
Chico, CA 95926

JULIAN BOND
Legislator, civil rights leader,
founder of the Student Nonviolent Coordinating Committee, Georgia state senator

The Center for Strategic and International Studies
Georgetown University / 1800 K Street Northwest / Washington DC 20006 / Telephone 202/887-0200
Cable Address: CENSTRAT
TWX: 7108229583

April 25, 1983

Dear Paul:

Thank you for your letter. I do believe in God. I do so because I think there is some deeper meaning to our life, which we cannot fully comprehend ourselves—just as we cannot fully comprehend the concept of infinity (that is, the absence of a beginning and the absence of an end).

With best regards to you,

Sincerely,

Zbigniew Brzezinski

Mr. Paul Rifkin
674 Rt. 6A
East Sandwich, MA 02537

ZBIGNIEW BRZEZINSKI
Government official, director of the Trilateral Commission
Assistant to President Carter for national security affairs

June 1, 1983

Mr. Paul Rifkin
Grade 6
674 Rt 6 A
East Sandwich, Massachusetts 02537

Dear Paul:

I am sorry to be so long in answering your letter, and I hope my reply is not too late for your report.

You ask a very important question, which deserves a serious answer. I do believe in God. It is harder to put in words why I believe in God and how he has made his presence known to me. I think the best answer I can give you is contained in the Gospel of St. John, Chapter 4 in which he writes that "Everyone that loveth is born of God and knoweth God."

I have been fortunate in family, friends and colleagues all of whom have at times revealed aspects of God.

I hope you are equally fortunate.

With best regards,

Sincerely,

Ellsworth Bunker

Ellsworth Bunker

ELLSWORTH BUNKER
U.S. ambassador to Vietnam (1967–73)

10/23/76   <u>Dear Paul</u>

Of course I believe in God—
He is a real presence in our lives.

Best regards

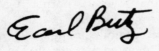

EARL BUTZ
Secretary of Agriculture under President Nixon

UNITED FARM WORKERS of AMERICA AFL-CIO
National Headquarters: La Paz, Keene, California 93531
(805) 822-5571

March 24, 1983

Paul Rifkin
674 Route 6-A
East Sandwich, Massachusetts 02537

Dear Paul:

Thank you for the letter you wrote to me on February 10, 1983. I am sorry that I could not answer you sooner, but many meetings with farm workers in California and additional engagements made it impossible.

I am pleased that you included me in the survey of people that you respect. My answers to your question will be brief, but I hope they will be satisfactory.

Yes, Paul. I definitely believe in God! The presence of God has been made clear to me first of all by my parents. My father (who died last October at the age of 101!) and my mother were good Catholics and brought us up with great respect for God. They made sure that we learned our prayers, that we respected the teachings of the Church, and that we tried to live justly.

Since I have grown up, the presence of God has been made clear to me in two different ways: through other good people who love God and their brothers and sisters so heroically (Gandhi, St. Francis of Assisi, Rev. Martin Luther King, Jr., Dorothy Day, Mother Teresa) and through my own personal prayer, especially meditation. I find that, if I provide time and silence for God, He will make his presence known to me.

As I said, my answers are quite brief, but I hope they will give you an idea of the presence of God in my life and they will be of use to you in your survey.

CESAR CHAVEZ
Union official—president of United Farm Workers of America

Good luck with the survey! I hope that you will always remember the cause of poor migrant workers and other oppressed people who suffer so much.

Viva la Causa!

Sincerely,

Cesar E. Chavez
President

CEC:ew

THE CITADEL

THE MILITARY COLLEGE OF SOUTH CAROLINA

CHARLESTON, S. C.   29409

GEN. MARK W. CLARK, U. S. A., RET.
PRESIDENT EMERITUS

18 April 1983

Mr. Paul Rifkin
Grade 5
674 Route 6A
East Sandwich, Mass 02537

Dear Paul:

Your letter has been received and I note your interesting survey you are making.

To answer your first question; yes, I do believe in God.

I cannot answer your second question with a definite statement as you have requested but I will tell you that as a little boy my family taught me to say my prayers and of more importance, to believe that they would be answered. During my long service in the Army, involved in combat in World War I, World War II, and Korea, I was in command of many soldiers, and responsible for their well-being and their very lives. I continued to say my prayers, knowing that they would be answered, and they were.

I hope you get a high grade on your interesting class report.

Sincerely,

Mark W. Clark

MWC:tp

MARK W. CLARK
Four-star general—chief of staff for ground forces in Europe, 1942

United States Senate

WASHINGTON, D.C. 20510

BOB DOLE
KANSAS

STANDING COMMITTEES:
AGRICULTURE, NUTRITION, AND FORESTRY
FINANCE
JUDICIARY
RULES

April 25th, 1983

Mr. Paul Rifkin
674 Route 6A
East Sandwich, MASS. 02537

Dear Mr. Rifkin:

Thank you for your letter concerning your survey of famous people.

I have always had a strong belief in God. Because of this I have been a consistent supporter of voluntary prayer in public schools and generally support any measure which, within constitutional boundaries, would restore the right of school children to the freedom of religious expression. These measures are pending in the Judiciary Committee of which I am a member.

Again, thank you for contacting me on this important issue. Please accept my best wishes for your academic success.

Sincerely,

BOB DOLE
United States Senator

BD:db

ROBERT DOLE
U.S. senator, Kansas

April 19, 1983

Dear Paul Rifkin:

I am a lifelong active Christian, an Episcopalian. So of course I believe in God. He has not been "revealed" to me, and I have never known anyone, even my fundamentalist parents, who actually had God revealed. My faith is based upon a complete understanding of both the Old and New Testaments, and constant study not only of the Bible but of helpful books about the Bible.

I accept much on faith, not on revelation.

Sincerely,

Milton S. Eisenhower

Mr. Paul Rifkin
Grade 5
674 Rt. 6A
East Sandwich, Mass. 02537

MILTON S. EISENHOWER
Retired president of Johns Hopkins University

English Department
Rutgers University
Newark, New Jersey 07102

Paul Rifkin
4212 - 25th Street
San Francisco, CA 94114

Dear Paul Rifkin,

Throughout history people have believed in many different names. My own belief is in the power of people to develop ourselves into a society of respect for one another right here on this earth. Slowly but surely human beings will wipe out injustice and poverty and there will be equal opportunity for each individual to develop his or her capabilities to the fullest extent. That way after a certain point each generation will advance beyond the previous generation. People will live in harmony with each other and with the universe, understanding more and more of life as time goes by. In short, there will be paradise on earth.

Thank you for your letter. I deeply appreciate your interest and wish you good luck with your survey.

Sincerely,

H Bruce Franklin

So many deeds cry out to be done,
And always urgently;
The world rolls in,
Time presses.
Ten thousand years are too long,
Seize the day, seize the hour!

The Four Seas are raging,
 clouds and waters raging,
The Five Continents are rocking,
 wind and thunder roaring.
Away with all pests!
Our force is irresistible.

 —from a poem by
 Mao Tse-tung

H. BRUCE FRANKLIN
College professor, political activist

The Farm
P.O. Box 156
Summertown, Tennessee
38483

Dear Paul

Yes I believe in God

God manifests in everything that we see in the whole world. The question is not what is God. The question is what is every thing and the answer is God. There is nothing which is not God.

Love

Stephen gaskin

STEPHEN GASKIN
Hippie leader of "The Farm"

BARRY GOLDWATER
ARIZONA

COMMITTEES:

INTELLIGENCE, CHAIRMAN

ARMED SERVICES
  TACTICAL WARFARE, CHAIRMAN
  PREPAREDNESS
  STRATEGIC AND THEATRE NUCLEAR FORCES

COMMERCE, SCIENCE, AND TRANSPORTATION
  COMMUNICATIONS, CHAIRMAN
  AVIATION
  SCIENCE, TECHNOLOGY, AND SPACE

INDIAN AFFAIRS

May 19, 1983

Mr. Paul Rifkin
Grade 5
G74 Route GA
East Sandwich, Massachusetts 02537

Dear Paul:

Thank you very much for your recent letter. In answer to your question "Do I believe in God.", I certainly do. I have always been guided by his presence and see his work in everything from the beauty of the sunsets in my own state of Arizona to the way this country has lived and thrived under freedom.

Sincerely,

Barry Goldwater

HON. BARRY GOLDWATER
U.S. senator, Arizona; Republican candidate for president (1964)

Assembly
California Legislature

Committees:
Vice Chair, Revenue
& Taxation
Economic Development
& New Technologies
Consumer Protection
& Toxic Materials
Education

TOM HAYDEN
Member, California State Assembly
44th District

Mr. Paul Rifkin
674 Route 6A
East Sandwich, Massachusetts 02537

July 20, 1983

Dear Paul,

Very few of us can <u>know</u> if God exists, but we can <u>believe</u> —and I do—that there is a creative force that is larger than all of us.

I was born and raised a Catholic, but in whatever way we think of God, it is a reminder that we are more than individuals, that there is a common bond of humanity that unifies us, and that we are responsible for one another.

That is a faith that can fulfill and sustain one over the years, a faith that can keep us going and searching, and makes life worth living.

Thanks for taking the time to write. Best wishes on your search for faith and fulfillment.

Regards,

TOM HAYDEN

TOM HAYDEN
Social activist, writer, legislator, cofounder of Students for a Democratic Society

E. HOWARD HUNT

Paul:

Yes, I believe in God.

I first felt His presence in the skies and the seas, the wonders of nature around us.

E. HOWARD HUNT
Author, retired government official—consultant to President Nixon

THE CITY OF NEW YORK
OFFICE OF THE MAYOR
NEW YORK, N.Y. 10007

October 15, 1980

Mr. Paul Rifkin
Grade 5
674 Route 6-A
E. Sandwich, Mass. 02537

Dear Paul:

Yes, I do believe in God. And God makes his presence felt every day simply by permitting me to awake each morning and do my job.

All the best.

Sincerely,

Edward I. Koch
Mayor

Domaine d'Argenteuil

1410 Waterloo, April, 28th, 1983.

Dear Paul,

His Majesty King Leopold has received your letter.
I am authorized to tell you that King Leopold believes in God.

As far as the second part of your question is concerned, you shall understand it is such a personal matter that the King prefers not to answer it.

With kind regards.

Colonel B.S.M. Baron van GAUBERGH.
Aide de Camp du Roi Léopold.

To Paul Rifkin
674 RT 6A
East Sandwich
Mass 02537
U.S.A.

KING LEOPOLD
Former monarch of Belgium

United States Senate

COMMITTEE ON
AGRICULTURE AND FORESTRY
WASHINGTON, D.C. 20510

HERMAN E. TALMADGE, GA., CHAIRMAN

JAMES O. EASTLAND, MISS.
GEORGE MC GOVERN, S. DAK.
JAMES B. ALLEN, ALA.
HUBERT H. HUMPHREY, MINN.
WALTER D. HUDDLESTON, KY.
DICK CLARK, IOWA
RICHARD B. STONE, FLA.
PATRICK J. LEAHY, VT.

ROBERT DOLE, KANS.
MILTON R. YOUNG, N. DAK.
CARL T. CURTIS, NEBR.
HENRY BELLMON, OKLA.
JESSE HELMS, N.C.

MICHAEL R. MC LEOD
GENERAL COUNSEL AND STAFF DIRECTOR

October 18, 1976

Dear Paul:

Thank you for your letter of October 12th.

Yes, Paul, I am a devout believer in God. I am also a frequent reader of the Bible which, for all my life, has been my greatest source of inspiration. As you may know, I am the son of a Methodist minister, so my religious training came early and intensively. I also studied for the ministry myself and in fact had my own congregation for a while before going into teaching—and from there, of course, into politics.

Thanks for writing to me, Paul, and I would be interested in seeing the results of your survey if you would be kind enough to send them to me when you have completed your research.

With every good wish, I am

Sincerely,

George McGovern

Paul Rifkin
4212 25th Street
San Francisco, CA 94114

GEORGE McGOVERN
Lawyer, former U.S. senator, South Dakota
Democratic candidate for president (1972, 1984)

8-7-83

Dear Paul—

I believe in God because of the beauty of the Universe. Only a loving creator would give us so much to enjoy—and so much challenge to keep.

Sincerely—

MAUREEN REAGAN
Daughter of President Ronald Reagan

June 21, 1983

Paul Rifkin
674 Route 6A
East Sandwich, Mass. 02537

Dear Paul:

Thank you very much for your letter. Although we received your letter too late to be of help in your project, you were certainly working on an interesting and important subject for your report.

The answer to your question is yes. I am reminded of the observation attributed to Voltaire, the French philosopher, who was asked the same question. He replied, according to the story, that if he were walking along a path and found a watch, he would assume that the watch would have been made by a watch-maker. It would not have simply come together by chance or accident. That is, I believe, a good way to look at the world and universe where we live. Your question also reminded me of the observation that "there are no atheists in foxholes." In other words, the circumstances of life sometimes lead people to different beliefs or views—including on the question you posed—than they perhaps otherwise would have had.

I wish you all the best in the years ahead.

Sincerely,

William French Smith
Attorney General

HON. WILLIAM FRENCH SMITH
U.S. attorney general

<u>Yes</u>

Through the wonders of the world I saw around me in my boyhood on a farm

HAROLD STASSEN
Lawyer, signer of United Nations Charter
Perennial candidate for Republican presidential nomination

October 19, 1976

Dear Paul:

Thank you for your recent letter. It was very thoughtful of you to write and ask if I believe in God.

As a young boy I was raised in a family that had Bible devotion at breakfast. My father and my mother read me Bible stories before I was able to even read myself and my grandfather and father carried me to the camp meetings in the summer at Indian Springs in Georgia as a little boy. In the panhandle of Florida was where I think I first found and came to know Jesus Christ.

Paul, I know from experience that God is alive and that Jesus saves. And I know that I, like many people, have been in the valley of the shadow of death, and I know that when I was there that I asked God to let me live if it be his will, but if it not be his will, that I cast my lot with Him.
I would say to you Paul, and to all young people, if you have Jesus Christ in your heart and in your soul then by the worldly standard that we sometime measure things you are a multi-millionaire.

As Governor, I have dedicated and re-dedicated my life to our Lord and Savior Jesus Christ. I can certainly say that being a christian has helped me to be a leader for the people of Alabama.

In closing, always remember if you have Jesus Christ in your heart and he has you in the hollow of his hand, you are whole. And I am whole.

Again, thank you for writing and give my best wishes to your teacher and your classmates.

Sincerely yours,

George C. Wallace

George C. Wallace
Governor

GCW:kct

GEORGE C. WALLACE
Former governor of Alabama

Dear Paul,
   Of course, I believe in God. Just look at the Universe.
   "THE FINITE MIND CANNOT UNDERSTAND THE
INFINITE"

EMANUEL KANT

SAM YORTY
Lawyer, former mayor of Los Angeles

ANDREW YOUNG
5TH DISTRICT, GEORGIA

Washington, D.C. 20515

RULES COMMITTEE

October 18, 1976

Master Paul Rifkin
4212 25th Street
San Francisco, California 94114

Dear Paul:

Thank you for your letter of October 10th regarding your class survey.

I am honored by your expression of respect for me and I will continue to strive to be worthy of your esteem.

You asked me about my belief in God, and I can truthfully answer you that I do believe in the Lord as the Creator and Giver of Life to this world. As you may not know, I am an ordained Minister in the United Church of Christ. Before I was first elected to the Congress in 1972, I worked with the Rev. Martin Luther King, Jr., in the social movement for human justice in America during the 1960's.

I have enclosed for you a short biography which may be of interest to your survey.

I appreciate hearing from you. Good luck in your studies.

Sincerely,

Andrew Young

Andrew Young
Member of Congress

ANDREW YOUNG
Mayor of Atlanta, Georgia; former U.S. ambassador to the United Nations

E. R. ZUMWALT, JR.
ADMIRAL, U. S. NAVY (RET.)

21 November 1980

Mr. Paul Rifkin
674 Rte. 6-A
East Sandwich, Massachusetts 02537

Dear Paul:

God first made His presence known to me in the battle of Surigao
Straits when the Japanese battleships had opened up on my destroyer
with their main battery guns. The first salvo was over. The second
salvo was short. The third salvo would have hit but, at that point,
our torpedoes hit them and our U.S. battleships opened up on them.
The Japanese shifted their fire and we were not hit. Afterwards,
we discovered that every man on our ship was praying at that moment.

I have not always been constant in my prayers, but I have found
that, in adversity, He is there and quite forgiving for my lapses.

All best wishes to you.

Sincerely,

E. R. Zumwalt, Jr.

1500 Wilson Boulevard
Arlington, Virginia 22209
703/841-8960

ELMO ZUMWALT
Retired naval officer, Asst. Secretary of Defense (1962–63)
Commander of U.S. naval forces, Vietnam (1968–70)

Businessmen

"I throw myself down in my chamber, and I call in and
invite God and his angels thither, and when they are there,
I neglect God and his angels, for the noise of a fly,
for the rattling of a coach, for the whining of a door."

—John Donne
"Sermons"

H&R Block, Inc.
Corporate Headquarters
4410 Main Street
Kansas City, Missouri 64111
(816) 932-8413

Henry W. Bloch
President and
Chief Executive Officer

February 14, 1983

Mr. Paul Rifkin
674 Route 6A
East Sandwich, MA 02537

Dear Paul:

Thank you for wiriting and asking for my opinion. Yes, I do believe in God and I feel he has had a strong influence in my life and career. His presence is constantly known to me in every major action I take, both businesswise and otherwise. If you are going to live your life as an upright citizen who always deals fairly with your fellow man, you must have a strong belief in God.

With kindest personal regards.

Very truly yours,

Henry W. Bloch

HWB:mam

HENRY BLOCH
President, H & R Block, Inc., tax consultants

193

THE GALLUP POLL

AMERICAN INSTITUTE OF PUBLIC OPINION

DR. GEORGE GALLUP
CHAIRMAN
GEORGE GALLUP, JR.
PRESIDENT
THOMAS REINKEN
EDITOR

November 15, 1976

Mr. Paul Rifkin
4212 25th Street
San Francisco, Ca. 94114

Dear Paul:

I was pleased to receive your letter. Your project is a very interesting one and I wish you luck.

To answer your question:

Yes, I believe strongly in God—a personal God whom we can reach in prayer. God's work is evident to me in nature, in the changing seasons, in life and death, the miracle of birth, and in love toward others. I believe that anyone can have a close relationship with God through prayer, sacrifice and an intense inner life.

I hope these remarks are helpful to you in your project. With best wishes,

Sincerely yours,

George Gallup, Jr.

P.S. You might be interested to know that I have a child who is in fifth grade, also. Her name is Kiki.

GEORGE GALLUP, JR.
Research organization executive—president, The Gallup Poll

LEE A IACOCCA

CHAIRMAN OF THE BOARD

CHIEF EXECUTIVE OFFICER

October 29, 1980

Paul Rifkin
674 Rte. 6-A
E. Sandwich, Mass. 02537

Dear Paul:

Thank you for your nice letter regarding a class report that you are preparing.

In answer to your question, yes, I do believe in God. I am a practicing Roman Catholic, I attend Mass regularly, and as is the case with most Christians, God revealed his presence to me through the scriptures.

Sincerely yours,

[signature]

LEE IACOCCA
Automotive manufacturer—president, Chrysler Corporation

10/12/80

Dear Paul,

Yes, I believe in God. I probably came to Him in childhood most strongly through my grandfather, Dr. Henry Winters Luce, who was a Presbyterian minister educator in China. His enthusiastic faith and pervasive goodness were a strong influence and example. I made the more intellectual commitment after a later teen-age period of questioning and doubt. I decided to affirm God as Creator, for I perceived that not to do so would leave me in a perpetual state of confusion and ignorance of the origin and purpose of the universe and life. It seemed obvious that we, mankind, would never be able to furnish an empirical explanation of this, and that, therefore, we had better hitch our star to an act of faith.

Sincerely yours,

Henry Luce III

HENRY LUCE
Publishing company executive—publisher, *Fortune* and *Time* magazines

Paul Rifkin
674 Rt. 6-A
East Sandwich, MA 02537

April 18, 1983

Dear Paul,

When I was a boy, I believed in God and continued my belief until I was 13 years old, when I was in my first year in high school and was introduced to the theory of evolution. Seeing the evidence as to how man has evolved from fish-like creatures and earlier from a single cell impressed me. But what convinced me was the growth of a human from a single cell to full development. During one stage of this development, the fetus has gills just like a fish. In a more advanced state, the fetus has a tail like a monkey.

One can trace the entire evolution of man from the single cell, through the fish and mammals, and finally to man, by studying the development of a human child before it is born.

Once I understood this, I no longer required the explanation of a supernatural being to explain the origin of life.

There are many mysteries that remain. But if you believe in a god, you need to ask who made god, and who made the being that made god? Believe only what can be observed or proven.

With all good wishes,

Nathan Pritikin

Nathan Pritikin

NATHAN PRITIKIN
Nutritionist—director, Pritikin Longevity Center

SARDI'S

April 22, 1983

Master Paul Rifkin
674 Route 6A
East Sandwich, Massachusettes 02537

Dear Paul:

I'm afraid I don't believe in the conventional God as taught by the various religious orders that I've come into contact with. I do feel that there's a "force" that does control and affect our lives and the universe. However, I do not feel that it has a beard or that it is a person of any kind. This will probably confuse you more than help you, but it is the best I can do in a brief letter.

Sincerely,

Vincent Sardi
VS:bab

VINCENT SARDI
Restaurateur—owner, Sardi's restaurant

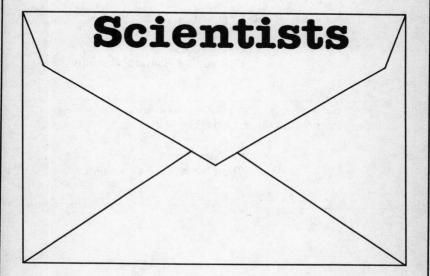

Scientists

"The universe is the language of God."

—Lorenz Oken
Elements of Physiophilosophy

"All our scientific and philosophical ideals
are altars to unknown gods."

—William James
The Dilemma of Determinism

MARY S. CALDERONE MD. MPH
NEW YORK UNIVERSITY
31 WEST FOURTH ST. 5 FL.
NEW YORK, NY 10003

June 1, 1983

Dear Paul,

That's an interesting question you ask, and I'll be looking to hear the results of your survey. How are you defining the word "famous?" How many people are you asking, how are you choosing them, the results you get? All that is called "setting the parameters," which means the rules, standards, boundaries, and other qualifications necessary in any survey.

You see, I am not only a medical doctor, but I have special training in public health. This always includes study of statistics, how to collect them, analyze and draw conclusions from them, and then make them known to the public. The people you will be questioning are part of that public, and have the right to know the answers to such questions, especially the very personal ones you are asking.

Now I'll answer your first question: yes, I most certainly believe in God as He is described in the New Testament by Jesus. I am a Quaker, and Quakers have a very special feeling about their relationship with God, and about all of the teachings of Jesus who based them on love of human beings as children of God. I have my Bible, given to me by a dear friend on my 14th. birthday, 1918. In it she wrote, "Let your light so shine before men that they will see your good works and glorify your Father who is in Heaven." That year I read the whole Bible through, and as I lived my life these past 65 years, I tried to use my scientific knowledge and what I have learned over the years about human beings and their needs, to be of help to them with some of the many difficult problems they meet in this great world.

The Quaker belief is that God works through people, that there is something of God in every person. I believe that, and I try to deal with people in that way. (By people I mean _e_v_e_r_y_o_n_e —babies, girls, boys, men, women), and I have many rewards: a loving family, (three children, two grandchildren and a third expected next November, and three great-grandchildren). And though I have not sought them I have been overwhelmed by the many honors and awards from universities and professional groups who understand what I am trying to do for people because I care about them. But the silver medals and honorary degrees framed on the wall are not to be compared to the love and caring I receive everywhere I go, from people I have never met but who recognize and thank me for my books, TV interviews and speeches which have helped them. Even on subways and in airports this happens, and that is more than enough reward.

That was all my answer to your second question. Your friend,

Mary S. Calderone MD

Mary S. Calderone MD

THE SALK INSTITUTE

April 20, 1983

Mr. Paul Rifkin
674 Route 6A
East Sandwich, Massachusetts 02537

Dear Paul,

No, I do not believe in God.

Yours sincerely,

Francis Crick

F. H. C. Crick

FHCC/bml

F. H. C. CRICK
Scientist—codiscoverer of double-helix structure of DNA

Institute for Advanced Study in Rational Psychotherapy

45 East 65th Street, New York, N.Y. 10021   (212) LEhigh 5-0822

30 March 1977

Paul Rifkin
Grade 5
333 W. Frances Willard
Chico, CAlif. 95926

Dear Paul:

In answer to your question, Do I believe in God? The
answer is certainly not. I am a probablistic atheist, and
believe that the probability of any God existing is exactly
the same as the probability of the existence of any fairy,
gnome, or hobgoblin. Such entities <u>could</u> exist but the
probability of their being extant and having power over
humans is about .000000000000001. Therefore, I choose
to believe that they do not exist and will sceptically
wait for evidence that they do. I expect quite a long wait!

Sincerely yours,

Albert Ellis

Albert Ellis, Ph.D., Executive Director

AE:mr

ALBERT ELLIS
Clinical psychologist
Executive director, Institute for Rational Living; Author—*Sex without Guilt*

HENRY J. HEIMLICH. M.D.
Professor of Advanced Clinical Sciences

April 5, 1983

Master Paul Rifkin
674 East Sandwich, MA 02537

Dear Paul:

Yes, I do believe in God. My belief may be different from yours, and different from someone's in China, Russia, India, or Egypt. My God does not look like a man with a flowing beard, who is always white. To me, God is a thought within our brain that we communicate to each other and through which we make choices as to how we shall live with one another. Should the leaders of the United States and the Soviet Union continue to make decisions to increase nuclear arms, then our choice will be to destroy all the people and their minds, and God will no longer be with us. I hope that you and all other children will convince your parents to make the governments stop fighting, just as they keep you and your friends from fighting. Life is a wonderful thing. Do not let the older people take it from you.

Sincerely,

Henry J. Heimlich, M.D.

HJH/ph

HENRY HEIMLICH
Physician, surgeon—developer of the Heimlich maneuver
(lifesaving technique for victims of food choking)

Dr. Robert Jastrow
Box 90
Hanover, NH 03755

April 15, 1983

Paul Rifkin
674 Route 6A
East Sandwich, MA 02537

Dear Mr. Rifkin:

Thank you for your recent letter.

My views on this question are those of the agnostic—the person who is not certain whether God exists. I do believe, however, on scientific grounds, that there is evidence for the existence of forces in the Universe that are beyond the power of scientific description.

I am enclosing a complimentary copy of a book I have written on related matters that may be of interest to you and your teacher.

Sincerely,

Robert Jastrow

RJ/na

ROBERT JASTROW
Physicist—head of the theoretical division of Goddard Space Flight Center, NASA
Author—*The Evolution of the Solar System*

National Aeronautics and
Space Administration

Lyndon B. Johnson Space Center
Houston, Texas
77058

OCT 20 1980

Mr. Paul Rifkin
674 Route 6-A
E. Sandwich, Massachusetts 02537

Dear Paul:

Thank you for your letter. My answer to your question is yes, I do
believe in God.

I have always accepted the existence of a Supreme Being. When I
was a child, I'm sure my belief stemmed from my parents'
teaching and influence. As I matured and became educated as an
engineer, my faith in God also grew.

My work in the space program continues to strengthen my belief
that our universe was planned. It is too well-ordered to have
emerged accidentally. We are able to send spacecraft to other planets
because of natural laws and the preciseness of movements and
relationships of those planets.

I believe this is the result of a Creator, a master planner. To accept
it as happenstance just doesn't make sense to me. My question
to you is: How can anyone gaze into a clear night sky full of stars
and then declare there is no God?

Best wishes for a good class report and for a happy, productive
life.

Sincerely,

Christopher C. Kraft
Director

CHRISTOPHER COLUMBUS KRAFT, JR.
Space administrator—director of NASA Johnson Space Center

Shanti Nilaya

A non-profit, non-sectarian organization
dedicated to the enhancement of life and growth
through the practice of Unconditional Love.

Founded by Elisabeth Kubler-Ross, M.D.

April 11, 1983

Paul Rifkin
674 Rt. 6A
East Sandwich, MA 02537

My dear Paul,

Thank you for your letter.

Yes, I do believe in God. It's not only that I believe in God; but I know that he exists, and to me, knowing and believing are two very, very different things.

I do not think all of us on this planet earth with so many billions of people could survive in this chaos and with our own negativity all over the earth if God would not interfere and help us to survive, help us to give us the courage to keep on keeping on. If he would not have created flowers, trees, birds, salamanders, rabbits, mountain tops, rivers and waterfalls, which give us peace, enjoyment when life seems to be a little too rough. I hope that answers your question.

With love and blessings for your project.

Elisabeth K. Ross, MD

Elisabeth K. Ross, M.D.

EKR/td

ELISABETH KUBLER-ROSS
Physician, Author—*On Death and Dying* and *Death—The Final Stages of Growth*

COLLÈGE

DE

FRANCE·

—

26/04/83

Dear Paul Rifkin,
The answer is: No.
   With best wishes.

xandæ Céii-Craux

CLAUDE LÉVI-STRAUSS
French anthropologist, Author—*Le Totémisme aujourd'hui*

209

ROLLO MAY, LTD.

98 SUGARLOAF DRIVE
TIBURON, CALIFORNIA 94920
415 435-3926

October 14, 1980

Paul Rifkin
Grade 5
674 RT 6A
E. Sandwich, MA 02537

Dear Paul:

In answer to your question, I do believe in God but it is not a God most people would recognize. God to me is the ground of meaning and being. He makes his presence known through everything about us and within us.

Best regards.

Sincerely,

Rollo May

Rollo May

RM/so

P.S. God should not be referred to as he. It certainly is as suitable to refer to him as she or it. Personal pronouns are not applicable in that area.

ROLLO MAY
Psychoanalyst, Author—*Psychology, Love and Will*

22 October 1980

Mr. Paul Rifkin
674 Rt. 6A
E. Sandwich, MA 02537

Dear Mr. Rifkin:

In answer to your letter, I must tell you
that I do not believe in God.

Sincerely,

Linus Pauling

LP:dm

Center for Studies of the Person

October 28, 1980

Paul Rifkin
674 Route 6A
East Sandwich, MA 02537

Dear Paul:

I have been away for many weeks, so I don't know just how long your letter has been on my desk.

In answer to your question, I would say that it seems clear to me that there is some sort of a force working through you and me and all of us and probably through the inanimate world as well, struggling to make the universe a more complete and perfect place. I think we are all part of that force, and each of us has our obligation in it.

Whether you wish to call this "God" or not, is up to you. I hope you keep up your searching inquiries.

Sincerely,

Carl R. Rogers, Ph.D.
Resident Fellow

CARL ROGERS
Psychologist, Author—*On Becoming a Person*
Professor at the Center for Studies of the Person, La Jolla, California

Dear Paul—

Yes—in part through
young boys who ask
impertinent questions

Rusty Schweickart
APOLLO 9

Mr. Schweickart wrote this along with his permission to use his response.

AND THE DEVIL VIA
RIFKIN IMPERSONATING
A 5th GRADER!

aboard "Carapace"
British Virgin Islands

May 20 1977

Dear Paul

    I guess I'm what you call a humanist. If I ever join a church it will be the Unitarian-Universalist Church. I believe in the idealistic and spiritual side of humanity and that what good a person does lives after him. I don't actively disbelieve in God and I'd never argue with a believer—I'd envy him. But I don't know whether God in the sense of a personality exists—I'm doubtful.

    Human beings are a naturally believing species, as is shown by religions and God all over the world. From a psychological point of view I'd say that this is derived from the small child's love of, trust in, and awe of his father

Sincerely

Benjamin Spock

BENJAMIN SPOCK
Physician, educator, Author—*Common Sense Book of Baby and Child Care*

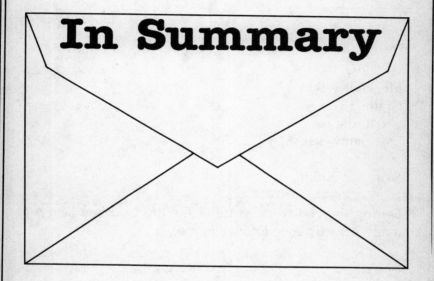

In Summary

ELIOT PORTER
ROUTE 4 BOX 33 SANTA FE NEW MEXICO 87501

29 May 1983

Mr. Paul Rifkin
Grade 5
674 Route 6A
East Sandwich, MA 02537

Dear Mr. Rifkin,

During the eightyone years of my life God has never made his existence known to me.

Sincerely,

Eliot Porter

ELIOT PORTER
Photographer, author—*American Places* and *In Wildness Is the Preservation of the World*

June 22, 1983

Dear Paul Rifkin—

Thank you for your letter of June 17th and I am happy to answer your question—I CERTAINLY <u>DO</u> BELIEVE IN GOD!

In fact, as far as I can recall I have believed in Him <u>all my life</u>. For that Gift of Faith, I am indebted to my dear Mother who was Superintendent of the Sunday School at the First Congregational Church of Mason City, Iowa and I can still remember sitting on her lap during church services when I was small.

I certainly hope when you are 81 years old as I now am you will have the same kind of lovely memory.

Sincerely,

Meredith Willson

Meredith Willson

MW:ldm

Mr. Paul Rifkin
674 Route 6A
East Sandwich, Mass. 02537